Your Conscience As Your Guide

For WESLEY and LUANNE who, as Lutherans, understand the relation of Law and Gospel; and for ROGER and JEAN, who, as Hebraists, understand the Grace of Law.

The biblical quotations are from the Revised Standard Version of the Bible, copyrighted © 1946 and 1952.

Copyright © 1984 Peter Toon

All rights reserved. No part of this publication may be reproduced, stored in a retrieval system, or transmitted in any form or by any means, electronic, mechanical, photocopying, recording, or otherwise, without the prior permission of the copyright owner.

Morehouse-Barlow Co., Inc.
78 Danbury Road
Wilton, Connecticut 06897

ISBN 0-8192-1339-X

Library of Congress Catalog Card Number 83-62870

Printed in the United States of America

Your Conscience as your Guide

Peter Toon

Morehouse-Barlow Co., Inc.
Wilton, Connecticut 06897

PB 419

Contents

Preface	9
Introduction	11
Who am I?	15
Whatever is my Conscience?	21
New Testament Foundations	33
Guilt, Forgiveness and Acceptance	41
Educating the Conscience	49
The Formation of Conscience	59
Training the Conscience	71
Conscience as Sovereign	79
The Function of Conscience	85
Free to Obey	91
Epilogue	99

Preface

Thoughtful and caring pastors, lay and ordained, tell me that they are noticing that Christian people want to discover afresh the place of conscience in their lives. This message coincides with my own observations.

In the last twenty or more years, churchgoers have been bombarded, perhaps invaded, by descriptions of conscience which are part of non-, or even anti-Christian systems of thought and moral values. Sometimes, in the name of modern knowledge, scorn has been poured upon the traditional Christian approach to the human conscience and the moral life of the Christian. Happily, we are beginning to wake up to the fact that, in the name of science and humanity, not a few people within our society are seeking to undermine its traditional Christian values and to introduce new values even into the churches. We are coming to see that we have come close to losing the precious reality of the concept of an educated Christian conscience.

Since I was so helped in the late 1950s by a simple book entitled *Conscience,* by the late Professor O. Hallesby of Scandinavia, I determined that I would try to provide something similar for the mid-1980s. His book was short and intended for students and busy lay Christians. So is mine. If mine is half as useful as his was, then I shall have much reason to thank God and my editor, the Reverend Theodore A. McConnell, who has given me much encouragement.

My wife has discussed the contents with me and helped me with the typing.

One final word. I have written the material in such a way that it has fit into ten chapters. In this way I hope that the work will be used and be useful for adult classes which like to take on a topic for ten weeks or so.

Peter Toon,
The Rectory, Boxford,
Suffolk, U.K.

September 1983

Introduction

On Wednesday, July 13, 1983, there was an important debate and vote in the British House of Commons. The issue, which caused great public interest and involvement was whether or not to restore the death penalty, which had been removed in the 1960s. The quality of the debate was high—the House of Commons at its best. The final vote by a decent majority was against the restoration of the death penalty on all counts, including the killing of policemen and prison officers.

Normally each member of Parliament is expected to vote as his political party directs. This is known as accepting the 'whip'; but, in this case it was a free vote, in that each member was expected to vote 'according to his conscience', without any pressure from the party. Thus the word *conscience* was used frequently before, during and after the debate, especially in the newspapers.

Writing in *The Sunday Times* of July 10, Hugo Young, the political editor, entitled his piece, 'Conscience is not enough'. Being convinced that the best arguments were against the restoration of the death penalty, Mr. Young was, however, worried that the right-wing conservatives would vote for the restoration, not because they were intellectually convinced that this was the right way, but because of their commitment to 'law and order' and to please their hard-line supporters. He wrote that not only is 'the conscience vote free and unwhipped', but 'it also runs the risk of elevating personal conscience above every other consideration: above reason, above evidence, above the broader social picture. Conscience, so rarely given rein becomes a kind of self-justifying guide, sufficient unto itself.' He feared that the 'conscience vote' would in fact be an excuse for prejudice and irrationality.

To be fair to Mr. Young (who wrote to me in explanation of his views), it must be said that he knew that in the Western tradition it has been clearly taught that the conscience is to be informed by the best reason and evidence so that it can distinguish right from wrong and make informed moral decisions and guide behavior. But his use of conscience was based on common usage in political circles —an irrational prejudice which has refused to study the evidence objectively. Moving from London to New York, I notice that in 1978 Paulist Press published a book entitled, *Don't let conscience be your guide*. In advertising it they explained that the author C. Ellis Nelson 'feels that if a man follows his conscience, he will make the moral choices his family taught or his society approves'. Here a Presbyterian educator used conscience as the repository of custom and conventional values.

To return to Britain, and to the debate over the restoration of capital punishment. In *The Sunday Telegraph* of July 17, Peregrine Worsthorne, its associate editor, who was strongly in favor of the restoration of the death penalty, wrote a piece entitled 'Fear of the rope'. He described the consciences of those both inside and outside Parliament, who were against restoration, as being either influenced by modern liberalism or refusing to face up to the moral demands of the day. So he wrote of 'the modern conscience' and the 'progressive conscience' possessed by those who had abandoned traditional values; and he spoke of 'the easy conscience' to refer to that state of mind which did not want to face the possibility of imposing the death penalty, preferring instead its own peace of mind of not having to feel guilty when a man went to the gallows.

Here we find that Mr. Worsthorne is well aware that the human conscience is both formed within a culture and society and informed by particular principles and rules. Thus, for example, the conscience may be informed by traditional Christian values and principles or by modern liberal and secular values. And to follow the conscience does not mean that the ensuing action is always right. So much depends on what principles are within the conscience as it decides what is right and wrong. Further, his reference to the 'easy conscience' reminds us that conscience often brings the sense of guilt, judging human actions. So we see that conscience functions both as judge and as guide of human behavior.

Crossing the ocean again, we can look to President Reagan for an example of the conscience as judge and guide. In 'Abortion and the Conscience of the Nation' (Spring 83 issue of *Human Life Review*), Mr. Reagan aimed to persuade his readers that the developing fetus in the mother's womb is truly a human life and therefore the principle of the sanctity of human life operates. He did not want his readers to have an easy conscience about the practice of abortion-on-demand. Rather he wanted them to feel guilty about the high rate of abortions in America and to feel responsible to work for an improvement in the situation.

Thus far we have noticed that 'my conscience' is used as the equivalent of 'the voice of my family's morals' (a usage found in Freud's psychology) and that it is also seen as the judge and guide of my moral life. However, we have also seen that conscience does not operate like a microchip—functioning identically in the microcomputer at all times in all places—but more like a sail on a boat, affected by the direction and force of the wind. What I am, and how I think, affects my conscience so that the way in which my conscience judges and guides cannot be separated from my total self, my approach to life, and my place within a given society and culture.

Perhaps two more examples will help to make this point clearer. Roman Catholic women appear to be quoted endlessly in the media saying, 'I have to follow my conscience and my conscience tells me that abortion is not wrong.' Here conscience is functioning as a guide, but it is guiding in the opposite direction to the teaching of the Roman Catholic Church. Such a statement is a kind of declaration of independence from authority. Here (unless it is a case of simple rebellion against Church teaching) that which guides the conscience is modern, liberal and secular culture.

Secondly, take the example of the well-educated young man from suburbia, who is very concerned about the poverty and deprivation of the inner city. So, he gives up good prospects and, at some personal risk, he goes to live and work in the inner city. People refer to him as having a 'social conscience', meaning that he feels an obligation to do something about the lot of those less fortunate than himself. In fact this young man could be either a Christian or a secular humanist for both are concerned about the welfare of the poor. Yet the conscience of the Christian would be informed by different principles than the humanist and their long-term goals would also be different.

We have emphasized that the conscience is to be judge and guide of the moral life. We have also seen that to be such the conscience has to be formed, informed and educated in such a way that it contains the genuine possibility of making a distinction between right and wrong and of guiding action into correct paths. This large view of conscience includes the possibility that I shall be told by my conscience that there are things I would like to do but ought not to do, and things that I do not want to do that I ought to do. It also requires that a Christian does all within his power to make sure his conscience is directed by the Lord Jesus Christ.

Such talk probably appears old-fashioned and out-of-date to some readers. They have been led to believe that 'conscience' is a kind of green light which tells a person to go right ahead and do what he or she really wants to do. It is that within the human person which continually gives permission 'to do your own thing'. This approach to conscience scorns the idea that my conscience has to be formed in accordance with objective, divinely-revealed truth. The erosion of the older idea of conscience as needing to be properly formed, and its replacement by this new idea of conscience as my right to do what I want, lies behind the serious erosion and decay of moral values in Western society. One of the problems of modern America, as well as Britain, is that too many of our people have malformed or badly-formed consciences. And, regrettably, they are not aware of this fact, or, if they are half aware, they do not want to put the matter right for they fear the obligations and restrictions that an informed conscience would bring.

The purpose of this book is to try to persuade Christian people that the Lord Jesus Christ desires that they allow him and his Church to educate their consciences so that they can live in the way he wants them to live.

1

Who am I?

My conscience belongs to me—it has no existence apart from me. Your conscience belongs to you and without you it is merely an abstract idea, an interesting thing to talk about. To have a clear view of what is conscience we must first be clear as to our identity: Who are you and who am I?

In western culture there are two main ways of understanding a human being. One way is to see man in the light of God and the supernatural: the other is to see man in the light of this world only. The Christian position is that a human being is a member not only of this world, but of another world (the kingdom of God) as well. In fact, the meaning of life in this world is derived from this other world, to which the Christian believes he is going after death. And this other world is where the Creator of this world is to be found in his full glory. In contrast, the secular humanist position either denies the existence of this other world, or treats it as if it had no existence. Thus it seeks the meaning of life only in terms of this world.

It has often been pointed out that the ancient paganisms and primitive Christianity had this in common—they held that the source of all things is a divine reality which transcends the world as well as operating within it. The secularisms of today have this in common—they hold that the meaning of this world lies within itself. Christianity and secular humanism are such different ways of evaluating the basic identity and meaning of human life, and each one is pervasive. Therefore, it needs no special argument to show that if my conscience is informed by secular humanism and yours by orthodox Christianity then they will operate on very different principles. For example, you will say, 'I ought to pray and to worship God as a priority', while I will feel no such moral compulsion. But in real life situations what we find is that Christians are affected by secular humanist principles and secular humanists are influenced by Christian principles. Most of the time such influence is through the society and culture and is diffused and implicit.

Having recognized this, it is important that we should not assume that humanism as such is contrary to Christianity. In his important book, *True Humanism* (1938), M. Jacques Maritain carefully distinguished between anthropocentric (= secularistic) and theocentric (= Christian) humanism. In theocentric or God-centered humanism the life of a human being is orientated not toward himself but toward his Creator and Redeemer, the Lord. This Christian humanism is the only form of humanism that does justice to the type of creature that man is, that offers satisfaction to his deepest needs and hopes, and that actually justifies the dignity which he believes himself to possess. Anthropocentric humanism is very influential today and is better called secular(ist) humanism. Part of its success is through its appeal to the achievements of science and technology; and its primary emphasis is that the only reality of which we need take any account is this world.

Strangely, and perhaps significantly, many of the top-line scientists are not secular humanists. Nevertheless, their contributions to modern life have caused the population at large to think that all our needs can be met by ourselves through our mastery of this world. And, in one way and another, this secular(ist) teaching reaches us each day through the media; and, it is so widespread and so much part of the cultural air we breathe, that much of it enters our minds without our realizing it. Because of this fact, Christians have to make a determined effort to allow themselves to be permeated by the ethos and principles of Christianity. Otherwise their minds will be secularist minds and their consciences will be malformed, even though they use Christian terms and attend worship. There is a battle for the education of the conscience being fought and secularist humanism is winning that battle right now. Christianity or theocentric humanism is losing simply because not enough time, energy and enthusiasm is being expended by Christians in the education of their consciences under the Lordship of Jesus.

I write these lines within the week of Pentecost 14 (Trinity 13) and the Collect in the Prayer Book of the Church of England for this week is this:

> Lord God,
> the protector of all who trust in you,
> without whom nothing is strong, nothing is holy:
> increase and multiply upon us your mercy,
> that you being our ruler and guide,
> *we may so pass through things temporal*
> *that we finally lose not the things eternal.*
> Grant this, heavenly Father,
> for the sake of Jesus Christ our Lord.

Too many in our generation are passing through things temporal in such a way as to lose things eternal. They think, live and act as though this world and what it contains (things temporal) are all that there is. Their lives and conversations give no indication that they want to reach out to God, his kingdom, grace and law (things eternal).

We need to be clear as to who we are as Christians in this world so that we can attend to the education of our consciences. Therefore I shall now try to provide a brief and simple answer to the basic question, 'Who am I?'

As Christians, we look to the record of God's revelation to mankind, recorded in the Bible, for the basis of the answer to this important question. Also, we look to the great Creeds of the Church (Apostles', Nicene and Athanasian) for guidance as to the way our fellow Christians of days past understood the teaching of the sacred Scriptures. From this source the answer we get is very different to what we are given by modern secularist thought. The basic Christian answer may be expressed in ten statements.

1. *I am God's creature.* Certainly God did not create me out of nothing. He created me in the womb of my mother from the egg fertilized by my father. So while I am the child of human parents, I am also God's creation. He made the whole universe in the beginning and he sustains the universe continually. As he sustains, so he also creates new life. I am part of God's total creation. God is the LORD and JUDGE of his world. As a creature I have a duty to worship God.

2. *I am a member of the human race.* I was not born a monkey or a goat but a human being. As such I am made 'in the image and likeness of God', having the ability to think, to love, to decide what is right and wrong and to relate to God in a personal way. Further, as a human being I am a member of the whole human race, for despite differences in color and facial characteristics, the human race is a unity. As a member of the human race I have a duty to treat others as I want them to treat me. As I wish to be treated with respect and concern, so I ought to treat others in that way.

3. *I belong to a particular family and nation.* I live in one type of family or another—the nuclear or extended or stem family. By blood or by adoption I have relatives. From these I receive honor and love and to them I feel an obligation. Further, I am a citizen of a country and this brings both privileges and duties. The will of the Creator and Judge is that there should be both families and nation-states: and, as a member of each of these, I have a duty to make them work effectively as just and caring units.

4. *I am a sinner.* Even though I try to fulfil my obligations to my family, my neighbors, my society and to my God, I fail to fulfil them as I know I should. Further, I recognize that I do not love God with my whole heart, soul, mind and strength and I do not have compassion for those in need who live around me. Without Christ, to stand in my place as my Representative and Substitute, I am a guilty sinner before the Lord, who is the Judge of the whole world. Knowing that I am a sinner, who breaks God's holy law, I ought to repent and believe the Gospel.

5. *I am baptized into Christ.* The external and visible sign that I am a Christian is my baptism, which I received from God's minister either as a child or an adult. My baptism is a sign that I have turned from sin to Christ and that I have been forgiven and accepted by God. It is also a sign that I am united to Christ, as my Representative, in death (death to sin) and in resurrection (to a new order of life). The fact of my baptism reminds me that my duty is to live as one who is baptized into Christ.

6. *I am a child of God.* God has adopted me, for Christ's sake, into his heavenly family. He has thereby given me brothers and sisters from all centuries, places and races for we all belong to the household of faith. Further, he has placed within my heart the Spirit of Christ to assure me of his love, to guide me through life, and to strengthen me to do his will. Because I am a child I can pray to my

heavenly Father and I know he will hear me. Because of all his mercy and grace toward me, I ought to seek to love him in return and live as he wishes me to live.

7. *I am a disciple of Jesus and under his Lordship.* By receiving the Gospel I entered the school of Christ to learn from Jesus Christ who I am and what my purpose in life is. In this school the Master is a perfect teacher and an infallible guide. The discipline in this school is tough and the way is often hard—for it is the way of the Cross— but having the world's best teacher it is also the best school to be in.

8. *I am a member of the kingdom of God.* Put another way, I live under the rule of the King of kings and Lord of lords. God is the Ruler of the whole universe: he is also the Ruler of the new creation that is being formed within the old creation. This emerging and new creation will be the reality which continues to exist after the judgment of the nations at the end of world history. As a Christian I am ruled by God within the old creation and within the new creation (of which I am a member by grace alone). Being under the fatherly and saving rule of God I ought to live in this world as one who longs to see his justice and righteousness operative in human affairs.

9. *I am a member of the one holy, catholic and apostolic church.* There is one Lord, one faith and one Church. This one Church is expressed locally as a Christian congregation, where the word of God is preached, the sacraments received, Christian fellowship enjoyed and service of God in the world initiated. United to Christ for salvation I am also united to his Church, and to its local expression, for worship, service and fellowship. Therefore I ought to be wholehearted in my support of, and commitment to, the local church. I cannot be a Christian in isolation.

10. *I am a pilgrim and my goal is the heavenly Jerusalem.* Knowing that I belong to Christ, to the kingdom of God and to the world above, I see my life on earth as a pilgrimage. My treasure is in heaven and not on earth and so I am not too concerned with the values of this world. My duty is to live as one who belongs to the age to come, the world above and beyond this world.

In one sentence, I am what I am by the grace of God.

In contrast to this Christian approach, the answer to the question 'Who am I?' from the secularist humanism of our day would be something like this: 'I am a human being, the most developed of the animals. I am to choose my own value system and code of morality.

I am not God's creature and there is no such thing as God's moral law. I am to use all the advancements in pure science, technology, and the social (behavioral) sciences to benefit myself and society. I am to choose when I die and whether or not to allow the fetus within me (if a woman) to grow into a human baby. I am to be as free as possible from all that restrains my self-expression and growth. Also I am to insist on my rights and the rights of others.'

Such emphases are common within society today and can be perceived behind the way that things are advertised, the contents of films, plays and novels and in the pragmatism that controls so much political, business, commercial and educational life. They, or similar ones, are set out in the *Humanist Manifesto II* (1973) which was signed by significant people, those who form opinion and create values in our society. Of moral values it declares:

> We affirm that moral values derive their source from human experience. Ethics is autonomous and situational, needing no theological or ideological sanction. In the area of sexuality, we believe that intolerant attitudes, often cultivated by orthodox religions and puritanical cultures, unduly repress sexual conduct. The right to birth control, abortion and divorce should be recognized.

Since 1973 the last sentence has been largely fulfilled. But the full impact of pure, secular humanism has not yet been felt in the West because we are still drawing on a bank account of Christian values and principles. However, this account will soon be overdrawn and then we shall perhaps see more clearly both the reality and force of secularist humanism and the need for Christians to think, live and witness as Christians. The trend—or march—of western society toward a culture that effectively denies God, his moral law and his grace, can only be reversed by the education of the consciences of those who are called Christians. They have to discard and reject that education of their consciences which is based on one or another brand of secularist thought and accept as replacement the Lordship of Jesus.

2

Whatever is my Conscience?

As yet, although we have discussed conscience, we have not said exactly what it is. The time has come to remedy the omission in two ways. First of all by identifying conscience in daily experience of life, and, secondly, by offering several definitions of conscience from Christian thinkers of different times and places.

IDENTIFYING CONSCIENCE

How do I know that I have a conscience? The answer is simple: I feel sure that I have a duty to do a particular thing or I feel sure that I ought to perform a particular action. Let us look more closely into this experience.

Each day you and I make many judgments. If something pleases us we say, 'It is beautiful' and if something is repulsive we say, 'It is ugly'. When you have food that you really enjoy, you say, 'This is terrific' or 'This tastes great'. As you go shopping you hear people remark, 'Isn't it cheap?' or 'That is very expensive' or 'Here is a real bargain'. As I write these pages I find myself saying to myself, 'This is a demanding job'. I'm sure that if you reflect on your experience of life you will recognize that you are often making judgments of one kind or another.

While making these varied judgments we sometimes make a special kind of judgment. In fact it is a unique kind of judgment. It is normally introduced by the word 'duty' or 'ought'. Perhaps you remember a friend telling you of a sick relative who was in hospital and then saying, 'I ought to go and visit her as soon as possible for she will have very few visitors.' Or, maybe, you are a parent with a child who needs correction. Though you are very hesitant to administer discipline you say to yourself or to your spouse, 'It is my/our duty to impose discipline for the child's own good.'

This moral judgment is also commonly expressed in statements about right and wrong. For example, a young man spends a morning helping an infirm, poor, old lady. She wants to give him money which she cannot really afford to give him. He says to himself, 'It is wrong for me to take money' and so he graciously refuses it. Or, a young woman is challenged to spend two years in voluntary social service in a deprived part of the Caribbean, and, feeling deeply about her obligation to go she says, 'It is right for me to go. It would be wrong of me to refuse to go.'

If you are a committed Christian then you believe that by saying, 'It is right' or 'It is wrong' and 'It is my duty' or 'I ought', you are claiming that the Lord requires you to act in a certain way. In fact you may sometimes use religious language instead of moral language and say something like this: 'The Lord has laid it upon my heart to go and visit my relative in hospital.' So Christians experience a feeling of duty either from the depths of their consciences or from the direct action of the Spirit of the Lord acting upon the conscience. This latter point will be taken up later (see chapter 8). Here what we need to note is that when people of all kinds experience the power and authority of conscience, the strength and force of its direction is not from outside but is from within. It is a part of me but it speaks with an authority that is greater than I personally possess. This is why it has sometimes (inaccurately) been called the voice of God within me, and why the Church has taught that conscience must always be followed/obeyed (*conscientia semper sequen da*).

The authority of conscience is revealed when what I feel sure I ought to do is in competition with both what I desire to do and what I believe is in my own self-interest. Two examples will help to clarify this point. Take the case of a reasonably happily married woman who meets an attractive man. He seems to have none of the failings of her husband and she is attracted to him. She desires to spend more time with him but she feels deeply that she ought to be faithful to her husband and to the vows she made before God and her church. Take, secondly, the case of a successful businessman who has a wife and two teenage children. It is Friday and he has been away all week doing his job. Then a phone call comes asking him to fly to Europe where there is a possibility that he will be able to clinch a profitable deal. He knows that his wife is under pressure and that his two teenage children need to see their father sometimes. He feels he ought to go home but he also is tempted to go after this deal in Europe. In each of these cases the person concerned could silence or ignore conscience. Yet in these experiences both the woman and the man know that the command of conscience is not lightly to be ignored or disobeyed.

Everyone has a conscience. It does not matter whether a person is a theist or an atheist, old or young, rich or poor, male or female; to him/her comes this experience of feeling 'I ought'. Of course this does not mean that what is felt to be duty is identical in all consciences of all people in all cultures. What is found everywhere is a sense of right and wrong; and, for many good reasons, what is judged to be right and wrong is not the same in all societies and cultures. A garden can be planted with many different vegetables and flowers or it can be left to the planting of seeds by wind and birds. Likewise a conscience judges what is right and wrong but how it judges depends on what is planted in it. This is why the education of the conscience of a Christian is so important.

Not only is conscience unique. Words used to express moral obligation are also unique. Such words as 'duty', 'ought', 'right', 'wrong', 'evil' and 'good' when used in moral judgments cannot be changed into other words. I may say that 'I ought to tell the truth' means the same as 'I must tell the truth' and think that I have contradicted this point. However, if I feel a duty to tell the truth then my 'must' is just careless grammar and means 'ought'. There are those who will try to tell you that all moral language is socially and economically conditioned and that it is basically no different from other types of language. But this is theoretical and not practical. Take the case of the man who claimed that all moral feelings were created by particular social and economic factors. One day he found his wife having an affair with another man and her excuse was, 'The economic position in which you are placed does not allow me to enjoy myself and so I go out with a man who can look after me in a way which pleases me!' Contrary to his principles, the man felt that his wife ought not to have behaved in this way and he told her so!

We live in days when psychologists may well be able to describe my or your moral feelings in great accuracy—much to our amazement. In fact it has been one of the great achievements of psychology to describe the moral and intellectual development of children as well as to relate guilt feelings in later life to the experiences of childhood. But, as any thinking person recognizes, there is a big difference between description and evaluation. To describe moral feelings and actions in psychological terms is not the same as to evaluate them in moral terms. When we have finished describing our actions and feelings they still have to be evaluated. And when we seriously begin to evaluate them we recognize that the sense of duty or obligation can never be wholly accounted for in terms of situation and context. The 'extra' dimension is what makes a moral judgment and feeling different to an economic or aesthetic or commercial judgment.

Because all human beings are sinful, plagued with the problem of gone-wrongness, they often try to avoid 'duty' and 'obligation' and also sometimes try to negate or explain away the reality of conscience as the origin of moral feelings and judgments. Those who are familiar with psychological accounts of conscience have probably noticed this tendency even in brilliant men and women. Great harm has been done to the basic morality of thousands of ordinary people through the dissemination (often in second-hand form) of theories of conscience which have the effect of diminishing or changing traditional moral values. Then there are the theories of some sociobiologists who claim that morality is merely the strong imprinting upon our human nature of built-in values which are intended to help us survive. Therefore to do what is right is only a way of 'fitting in with the process and direction of evolution'. We cannot discuss these theories here. It is sufficient to say that Christians need to be aware that all kinds of views are being taught today which undermine the Christian idea of morality.

The language of 'I ought' and 'my duty is . . .' points to the function of conscience both as judge and guide. We have feelings of guilt when we have not done what we ought to have done. How often people say, 'It was my duty to have done this or that and I feel bad about it now.' And the greater our knowledge of duty, then the more we are likely to fail and thus feel guilty. This is why the

Christian doctrine of forgiveness is so important for it relates practically to people in such a state of mind.

Before moving on to notice how the conscience is defined by the experts, there is one further indication of the existence of conscience worth observing. We have seen how the conscience speaks clearly by saying, 'This is right' and 'This is wrong' and 'You ought to do that'. Such internal convictions may be called *preceptive* for they give a command to be obeyed without further questioning. However, careful self-examination reveals that the conscience sometimes functions in a *permissive* way, giving freedom to do this or that but not commanding that anything be done.

The words I normally use when my conscience permits me to act in a certain way are 'I may do this' or 'I can do this'. For example, a general problem faced by young people from evangelical backgrounds is, 'May I drink beer or wine?' The answer from an educated conscience would probably be, 'Yes, you may drink beer and wine.' However, a declaration of my right or liberty to do a thing, does not mean that I ought to do it. Take another example. A widow or widower faces the question, 'May I remarry?' An enlightened conscience would probably say, 'Of course you may remarry.' But the liberty to remarry does not imply the duty to remarry. Eventually 'I may do this . . .' usually becomes 'I ought to do this . . .' or 'I ought not to do this . . .', as a real choice has to be made. A final comment is necessary. The person with the educated conscience never gets into the habit of asking 'What may I do?' rather than 'What ought I to do?' The 'May I?' arises but not so often as the 'Ought I?' For example, a pregnant woman should not ask, 'May I have an abortion?' Rather, the question is 'Is it my duty to have an abortion?'

DEFINING CONSCIENCE

Within the Christian tradition, Protestant and Catholic, for a thousand or more years conscience has been defined in terms of (1) recognizing and seeing moral truths as true and binding, and (2) applying these truths to particular situations—e.g. the truth that it is wrong to kill to the practice of euthanasia or abortion. The great medieval philosopher and theologian, Thomas Aquinas distinguished between *synderesis* by which he meant recognizing moral truth and *conscientia* by which he meant applying moral truths to personal situations. But, since his time it has become common to use *conscientia* (conscience) to refer to both aspects of making moral decisions and choices. For more detail on this development of the meaning of conscience the reader is advised to look at C. E. Curran, *Themes in Fundamental Moral Theology,* 1977, chapter 8 on 'Conscience'.

Those who are familiar with the English Puritan tradition will know that some Puritans were experts on the analysis of conscience and on the solving of cases of conscience (= casuistry). They made much use of what they called the *practical syllogism,* for they held that it reflected how conscience moved from the general to the particular. A simple example of a practical syllogism is the following:
1. To covet is wrong.
2. Fervently desiring to possess the books in my neighbor's library is coveting.
3. Therefore, I ought not feverently to desire to possess the books.

This method can still be helpful but since the use of the syllogism is virtually non-existent in the way we express ourselves today, it is perhaps best to forget it. Perhaps the best known example of Puritan writing on the duties of conscience is the massive, *The Christian Directory* (1675) by Richard Baxter (1615–1691), parts of which appeared in Everyman's Library in 1925.

For a powerful description of the conscience of a Christian from Puritanism, we turn to Richard Sibbes (1577–1635). Preaching from 2 Corinthians 1:12 which includes the words 'testimony of our conscience' he described its operation with the help of the working of a court.

> Know that God has set up in a man a court, and there is in man all that are in a court. 1. There is a *register* (= registrar) to take notice of what we have done . . . The conscience keeps diaries. It sets down everything . . . 2. And then there are *witnesses.* 'The testimony of conscience'. Conscience doth witness, this I have done, this I have not done. 3. There is an *accuser* with the *witnesses.* The conscience it excuseth or accuseth. 4. And then there is the *judge.* Conscience is the judge. There it doth judge, this is well done, this is ill done. 5. Then there is an *executioner,* and conscience is that too . . . The punishment of conscience, it is a prejudice (= pre-judging) of future judgment. . . .
>
> God hath set and planted in man this court of conscience, and it is God's hall, as it were, where he keeps his first judg-

ment . . . his assizes. And conscience doth all the parts. It registereth, it witnesseth, it accuseth, it judgeth, it executeth, it doth all. [*Works,* 1862, vol.3. pp210f.]
Though we may judge that the analogy is pushed too far, we must recognize the high doctrine of conscience it presupposes.

Moving from the seventeenth to the eighteenth century we turn to the published sermons of Bishop Joseph Butler (1692–1752), who is most famous as the author of the *Analogy of Religion,* but who made his reputation in England through his preaching in the Rolls Chapel, London. In the first sermon of his collection of *Fifteen Sermons* he has this to say about conscience:

> There is a principle of reflection in men, by which they distinguish between, approve and disapprove their own actions. We are plainly constituted such sort of creatures as to reflect upon our own nature. The mind can take a view of what passes within itself, its propensions, aversions, passions, affections, as respecting such objects, and in such degrees; and of the several actions consequent thereupon. In this survey it approves of one, disapproves of another, and towards a third is affected in neither of these ways, but is quite indifferent. This principle in man, by which he approves or disapproves his heart, temper, and actions is conscience; . . . And that this faculty tends to restrain men from doing mischief to each other, and leads them to do good, is too manifest to need being insisted upon.

And in the second sermon he gave another definition:

> There is a superior principle of reflection or conscience in every man, which distinguishes between the internal principles of his heart, as well as his external actions: which passes judgment upon himself and them; pronounces determinately some actions to be in themselves just, right, good; others to be in themselves evil, wrong, unjust; which, without being consulted, without being advised with, magisterially exerts itself, and approves or condemns him the doer of them accordingly: and which, if not forcibly stopped, naturally and always of course goes on to anticipate a higher and more effectual sentence, which shall hereafter second and affirm its own . . . It is by this faculty, natural to man, that he is a moral agent, that he is a law to himself . . .

The emphasis in these quotations is on the function of conscience as judge but its work as guide is implied.

Moving now into the nineteenth century, we must quote that marvelous description of conscience supplied by John Henry Newman, who began as an evangelical minister of the Church of England and ended as a Cardinal of the Roman Catholic Church. In a published *Letter to the Duke of Norfolk* he said this:

> Conscience is the aboriginal Vicar of Christ, a prophet in its informations, a monarch in its peremptories, a priest in its blessings and anathemas: and even though the eternal priesthood through the Church should cease to be, in it the sacerdotal principle would remain and would have a sway.

This comes from his Roman Catholic period—thus the interest in the ministerial priesthood.

Though various winds of change blew through the Roman Catholic Church in the 1960s, they did not affect the definition of conscience. Here is a statement about conscience from the *Pastoral Constitution on the Church in the Modern World* published from the Second Vatican Council in 1965. Paragraph 16 of chapter 1 of this document is entitled 'The dignity of moral conscience' and it states:

> Deep within his conscience man discovers a law which he has not laid upon himself but which he must obey. Its voice, ever calling him to love and to do what is good and to avoid evil, tells him inwardly at the right moment: do this, shun that. For man has in his heart a law inscribed by God. His dignity lies in observing this law, and by it he will be judged. His conscience is man's most secret core, and his sanctuary. There he is alone with God, whose voice echoes in his depths. By conscience, in a wonderful way, that law is made known which is fulfilled in the love of God and of one's neighbor. Through loyalty to conscience Christians are joined to other men in the search for truth and for the right solution to so many moral problems which arise both in the life of individuals and from social relationships. Hence, the more a correct conscience prevails, the more do persons and groups turn aside from blind choice and try to be guided by the objective standards of moral conduct. Yet it often happens that conscience goes astray through ignorance which it is unable to avoid, without thereby losing its dignity. This cannot be said of the man who takes little trouble to find out what is true and good, or when conscience is by degrees almost blinded through the habit of committing sin.

And, in another document *The Declaration on Religious Liberty* (1965), the Council declared in chapter one:

> It is through his conscience that man sees and recognizes the demands of the divine law. He is bound to follow this con-

science faithfully in all his activity so that he may come to God, who is his last end. Therefore, he must not be forced to act contrary to his conscience. Nor must he be prevented from acting according to his conscience, especially in religious matters.

Here the priority of conscience is clearly affirmed.

In the *Dictionary of Christian Ethics* (ed. J. MacQuarrie), Ronald Preston defines conscience in this way: 'Conscience is a judgment of the practical reason at work on matters of right and wrong. There is an element of emotion in the workings of conscience because when the reason decides what ought to be done we feel emotionally drawn toward it, or emotionally divided if we partly shrink from doing it. In the same way if the moral reason passes judgment on what has been done we feel either 'pangs of conscience' or feelings of approval, whichever way the judgment goes.' In a symposium by British evangelicals on the topic of law and morality, James I. Packer defined conscience in this way: 'Practical moral reason, consciously exercized, growing in insight and sureness of guidance through instruction and use, and bringing inner integration, health and peace to those who obey it' (*Law, Morality and the Bible,* ed B. N. Kaye, 1978, p. 178).

Having looked over these definitions, you may perhaps feel that they rightly emphasize reason (practical and moral reason) and under-value the emotions (feelings and impulses), which are part of conscience. There is truth in such an observation. In fact, whenever definitions are framed there is a tendency to emphasize that which can be the more easily described—reason. However, the experience of living and choosing makes us aware that my conscience is I, myself, as a being with both moral consciousness and conscientiousness, expressed in thought, impulses and emotions. It has often been pointed out that sometimes it is probably nearer the mark to say 'a person is a conscience' than 'a person has a conscience'. Whatever we mean by conscience, precisely this reality cannot be taken away from us without our ceasing to be (either temporarily or permanently) less than normal human beings (a demoniac, or someone with a major psychiatric disorder). It has also often been pointed out that while I may say, 'My conscience directs me to . . .', I never say, 'My conscience directs you to . . .' Your conscience is yours and yours alone and mine belongs only to me. It is a unique aspect of your and my personhoods.

To conclude this chapter it will be well if we note various ways of looking at conscience (all found in our society) which we must reject.

1. *Always and in all situations conscience is God's voice within me and must be obeyed.* Here is a partial truth. Your conscience is your capacity for hearing God's voice rather than being God's voice itself (see below, chapter 8). Only as your heart and mind have absorbed the will of God can your conscience be said to be God's voice!

2. *Conscience is that aspect of me which reflects the customs, taboos, principles and prejudices of the family and society in which I was raised. It is not what I believe is right and wrong but what has been put in me by indocrination.* If this is what you have been led to think about conscience, then you are already sitting in judgment upon it, and so you are recognizing that your conscience is more than that which you were told was right and wrong as a child.

3. *Conscience is what Sigmund Freud called the super-ego.* It is certainly possible for a mentally sick or an imbalanced person to confuse (what Freud calls) his super-ego (the desperate compulsion to experience himself as lovable) with what Christians have traditionally called conscience. This is because repressed prohibitions and threats, internalized in childhood, can appear as powerful impulses to follow and can cause great pain and disturbance. The work of the psychotherapist is to help a patient strengthen his ego and view the contents of the super-ego for what they really are—traumas and nightmares of the past. So we see that Freudian psychology does help us to understand such things as the obsessional neurosis of the so-called 'scrupulous conscience'. For centuries the moral theologians of the Church have known of the 'scrupulous conscience' and it is treated in old text-books under the heading of 'scrupulosity'. The point to be made here is that while conscience may be affected by phobias, fears or frights of childhood, it cannot be defined in terms of them.

4. *Conscience is a conditioned reflex.* This is the doctrine that though I may think that I am making a choice, I am in fact working in much the same way as a computer and simply doing what I have been programmed to do by my heredity and early environment. This way of thinking is associated with behavioristic psychology. For example, in his book, *Beyond Freedom and Dignity,* Professor B. F. Skinner portrays human actions as essentially the result of psychological stimuli rather than of free and reasoned decisions.

I do not want to give the impression that psychology cannot be helpful to the wise pastor and counselor. For those who wish to stretch their minds and see how the insights of developmental psychology (to which we shall refer in chapter 6) can be harmonized with principles taken from philosophical theology to produce a modern definition of conscience, then the best book is Walter E. Conn, *Conscience: Development and Self-Transcendence* (1981). It points forward from the moral confusion within the Church (caused in part by the reception of half-baked psychological concepts and practices and by the lack of knowledge of moral theology in the Christian tradition, where conscience is much discussed) to the possibility of clearer thinking and better systems of ethics.

3

New Testament Foundations

One fact needs to be made clear as we approach the New Testament and the use of the word *syneidesis* (= conscience) in its books. The way in which conscience has been used in traditional Christian, moral language is broader than its use within the books of the New Testament. The difference is this. In the New Testament conscience refers primarily to a witness within human beings which creates a sense of pain (guilt) or pleasure (peace) with reference to past actions; in contrast, in Roman Catholic and Protestant theology conscience refers also to what ought to be done, today and tomorrow. In the New Testament conscience functions as the judge of past action, approving or disapproving, giving a red or green light; in later Church theology conscience functions in this way and also as the guide of what action is right for the future. In other words, the actual word, conscience, has expanded its reference from the judge of past action to the guide of future action as well.

This process of enlargement of meaning happened because the word conscience took into itself meaning that was conveyed by other words and concepts. In the New Testament Christians were told that they were to do what God wanted them to do and thereby to please him by loving what he loved and hating what he hated. They were urged to allow the mind of Christ to be formed in them: they were told to let the word of God dwell richly in their hearts to guide them: they were instructed to allow the Spirit of the Lord write the law of the Lord in their hearts and minds, and they were told to follow Christ and his apostles. Before I can determine by God's grace to follow Jesus I must have ideas in my mind as to what following Jesus is all about. It is this aspect of feeling that 'I ought to follow Jesus' and 'it is my duty to follow Jesus' and working out how I should do it, that Christian theologians discerned was implied by the reality of conscience. So they used the word in this larger sense as judging the past and guiding the future by the will of God.

If you remember this development of meaning you will not be confused or upset when you find a Christian scholar writing or saying this kind of thing:

> Conscience is not enough ... The wise Christian will give due weight to conscience: it is the natural reaction of his whole being as it has been developed under Christian influences. He will realise that by disobeying conscience he may be in danger of destroying himself. Yet he will turn more confidently to other, more objective and reliable, standards, which he can fully and reasonably accept as his own—the Word of God and the example of Christ ... [This is from William Lillie, *Studies in New Testament Ethics*, 1961, page 56.]

Here he is working with a narrow definition of conscience (which he believes was also held by St. Paul) and saying that it is not enough. Then he says that Christians must turn from conscience (as merely a witness within which condemns sin and failure) to follow more objective and reliable standards such as the teaching within the Bible and the example of Christ portrayed there. The answer to Dr. Lillie is that the concept of the conscience as guide means that what I feel and know that I ought to do (or what is my duty) is formed through my reading and study of the moral teaching contained in the Bible. I cannot follow the will of God written in Scriptures unless I first understand it and then apply it to the situation in which I find myself. I fear that such statements as this by Dr. Lillie have sometimes been influenced by modern psychological accounts of conscience; further, I suspect that they have done harm in the churches—especially amongst students of theology—by contributing to the demise of concern for the moral life.

At the risk of over-emphasizing this point, here is how the *New International Dictionary of New Testament Theology* (ed. C. Brown, vol.1, p. 353) explains the distinction between the narrow (limited) and large (extended) views of conscience:

When we speak of conscience in English, our meaning often seems to oscillate between conscience (1) in the narrow sense as the pain, or the instrument which makes us feel pain, when we transgress the moral law, and (2) in the wider sense of moral consciousness. The latter involves the whole person viewed as a rational being. It is not just the pain which works retrospectively in the light of past actions and which by extension might enable us to forecast what future actions might cause us pain. It includes the power of discernment and rational reflection which enables the mind to analyze situations and actions, to discern moral values and principles, the capacity to hear and apply the Word of God to our lives—and also conscience in the narrow sense. For the Christian, guidance belongs to the realm of moral consciousness in this wider sense which includes *syneidesis* in the narrower sense, but is by no means confined to it.

Here, Dr. Brown is comparing the concept of conscience taken over by Paul from its general use in everyday Greek (a concept which Paul refined) with the much later traditional Christian idea of conscience which we discussed in the last chapter.

Before turning to the New Testament, a brief word about the Old Testament is necessary. There is no special word in the Old Testament for the phenomenon of conscience, either in the narrow or wider meanings. Yet the Israelites knew what it meant to be guilty before God, to feel an assurance that they had done God's will, and to know that they ought to live each day by God's commandments. These various feelings (together with knowing and willing) are associated with the *heart* (Hebrew, *leb*). The pain of guilt is reflected in such statements as 'David's heart smote him' (1 Sam 24:5), and in his famous prayer, 'Create in me a clean heart, O God, and put a new and right spirit within me' (Psalm 51:10). In contrast, Job could look back over his relationship with God in his crises and claim: 'My heart does not reproach me for any of my days' (27:6). This feeling of a clear conscience is also conveyed by such expressions as 'uprightness of heart' and 'integrity of heart' (see e.g. Gen 20:5-6; Deut 9:5; 1 Kings 3:6; 9:4; Psalm 119:7). This comprehensive use of the word, heart, is also found in the New Testament, which though written in Greek often points to Hebrew ideas and usages. On several occasions, however, 'heart' seems to mean 'conscience' (e.g. Mark 8:17; Acts 2:37).

Syneidesis was apparently a reasonably common word in the Greek spoken in the Roman Empire. Its normal meaning was 'the pain or guilt felt by a person when he believes he has done wrong'. But it was one of those words which had not been given a precise meaning by the great philosophers of Greece. It occurs thirty times in the New Testament, never in the Gospels and most frequently in St. Paul's letters. In these epistles Paul's use of the word suggests that he saw conscience as the inward witness and judge of conduct according to norms implanted by God. So he could speak both of a good and bad conscience, of a clear and evil conscience. His use of conscience is of a present experience looking back critically over past action, approving or condemning. For a Christian a good conscience means that he feels that his life has been lived for the sake of the Gospel. At times Paul's usage suggests the possibility of conscience as guide of the present and future (e.g. Rom 13:3; 1 Cor 10:25) but this side is not developed.

Let us briefly note how Paul uses the word *syneidesis*. This may be conveniently summarized in four parts:

1. *The universal existence of conscience.* In Romans 2: 14-16 Paul wrote these words:

> When Gentiles who have not the law [of Moses] do by nature what the law [of Moses] requires, they are a law to themselves, even though they do not have the law. They show that what the law requires is written on their hearts, while their consciences also bear witness and their conflicting thoughts accuse or perhaps excuse them . . .

Gentiles did not possess the written Torah, the Law of Moses. Paul, however, insisted that when Gentiles recognized that they were truly God's creatures and sought to render to him the worship and obedience that creatures ought to give to their Creator, then they actually began to do what the Law required. The apostle believed that there is something within human beings, which should, and sometimes does, lead them toward an attitude of humble, sincere worship and obedience. When they behave in this way they show the effect of moral law, written on their hearts. Paul introduced conscience, not so much as the sphere where judgment takes place, but as a major witness, which may be called on either side—for God or for man—as the case requires. In this personification of conscience as the internal moral witness of human beings everywhere, Paul was teaching what philosophers of East and West have taught—the universality of the faculty which distinguishes right and wrong.

2. *A clear and good conscience.* Some members of the congregation of Christian believers in Corinth felt that Paul's activities had been strange and inconsistent. In explaining to them the action of his colleagues and himself he wrote: 'For our boast is this, the testimony of our conscience that we have behaved in this world, and still more toward you, with holiness and godly sincerity, not by earthly wisdom, but by the grace of God' (2 Cor 1:12). Though he does not use an adjective with conscience it is obvious that he and his friends had a good conscience, that did not bring them any sense of guilt.

Later in his ministry, when giving advice to the young man, Timothy, Paul spoke of the need to live by the power and teaching of the Gospel and to have a 'good' and 'clear' conscience. He told Timothy: 'the aim of our charge is love that issues from a pure heart and a good conscience and sincere faith' (1 Tim 1:5); 'wage a good warfare, holding faith and a good conscience' (1 Tim 1:19) and 'hold the mystery of the faith with a clear conscience' (1 Tim 3:9). Perhaps a 'good' is a stronger certainty than a 'clear' conscience. The first points to an internal assurance of complete loyalty to Christ and the Gospel.

3. *A weak or partially-formed conscience.* To become a Christian is the beginning of an education, including growth in knowledge, wisdom and obedience. So the conscience of the mature Christian should be better informed by the Gospel and the will of God than that of a new Christian (who has to unlearn what is contrary to the will of God and also receive the contents of God's revealed will). In writing to the church in Corinth Paul had to face the question of how to treat Christians with weak, partially-formed or even imbalanced consciences. The issue was whether or not to eat meat which had originally been offered as a sacrifice to a pagan deity. When animals were sacrificed to a god, the priests took what meat they needed; then the rest was usually sold in the meat market along with other meat, not from temple sacrifices.

Those Christians who fully understood the meaning of 'there is only one god' realized that idols were merely of stone, wood or metal and had no supernatural or natural life in them. Thus they were quite free to eat meat that had been offered to idols—for, among other considerations, it was good meat (only the best animals were used in temple sacrifices). Other Christians, converts from pagan idolatry and polytheistic culture, had genuine scruples about buying and eating such meat and were offended by Christians who ate it. In the one case the mature conscience did not judge as guilty but in the other case the weak conscience did judge as guilty.

What Paul wrote in 1 Corinthians 8:1-13 and 10:23—11:1 should be carefully read. The word 'conscience' occurs seven times. The apostle recognized that Christians were free to eat meat offered to idols, but he maintained that the freedom was controlled by the love of Christ: therefore, they must give due consideration to the people with weak, or tender, or partially-formed consciences; also they must not give any suggestion that they approve of, or support, idolatry. So, in order for a Christian to enjoy a clear conscience, he must restrict his own freedom in order to affirm the dignity of his weaker brother or sister—by not doing what his own conscience approves and what the conscience of the weaker brother forbids.

4. *An evil conscience.* Paul warned Timothy (1 Tim 4:3) that the churches would face problems in the near future. Members would be led away from true faith through 'the pretensions of liars whose consciences are seared' (literally 'who are cauterized as to their own consciences'). The apostle was a careful student of human nature and he knew that it was possible by constantly going against what one knows to be right and by stifling the constant warnings of conscience, to arrive at a position in which the conscience hardly functions as the judge of right and wrong and inflicts little or no pain.

Writing to Titus, Paul declared that 'to the pure all things are pure, but to the corrupt and unbelieving, nothing is pure; their very minds and consciences are corrupted' (1:15). Here he was referring to those who had rejected the Gospel of Christ; they had preferred darkness to light, and, as a result, their minds were filled with wickedness and evil principles, so that their consciences were corrupted in their judgments. So an evil conscience is found in a person who has definitely rejected the living God, his law, grace and Gospel. For in rejecting the truth, such a person has rejected the possibility of a clear conscience, having opted for its opposite.

If we now leave the writings of St. Paul and turn to the anonymous Letter to the Hebrews then we encounter the theme of guilt and forgiveness, and of a purified or perfected conscience.

5. *The purified and perfected conscience.* The Letter to the Hebrews compares the way to God and his salvation under the Mosaic, Old Covenant with that under the New Covenant, showing the superiority of the latter, centered in Jesus.

Under the Old Covenant animal sacrifices were offered in the Temple which could not 'perfect the conscience of the worshipper' (9:9). Only the sacrifice of Christ, his sacrificial blood, offered to God through the eternal Spirit can purify the conscience 'from dead works to serve the living God' (9:14). Thus the author, thinking of Jesus as the Priest who had offered the perfect sacrifice for sin and was now in heaven to represent his people to the Father, wrote: 'Let us draw near (to God) with a true heart in full assurance of faith, with our hearts sprinkled clean from an evil conscience...' (10:22).

The only remedy for a guilty or evil conscience (that recognizes that it is in a totally wrong relationship with God, the Judge) is the forgiveness of God made possible and freely bestowed through the sacrificial blood of Christ, who died and is alive for evermore. A purified or perfected conscience comes not through human endeavor but as the free gift of God's forgiveness in Christ. For he is the Lamb of God who takes away the sin of the world. And the only way to serve God freely and joyfully and to do what he loves and approves is with a purified, clear conscience, from which the burden of the guilt of sin has been removed.

We recall that Paul claimed he had a clear and a good conscience (Acts 23:1 and 24:16); he had experienced through his encounter with the exalted Lord Jesus on the road to Damascus both the feeling of guilt and the feeling of forgiveness and acceptance. His aim in life thereafter was to have a good conscience which functioned in perfect harmony with the indwelling, guiding Spirit of the Lord Jesus (Rom 9:1).

As was made clear above, *syneidesis* in the New Testament is the internal witness to, or judge of, past actions, seen from the perspective of the present according to norms received and believed in the heart. Thus it witnesses as clear or guilty, and it is either good (functioning by right norms) or bad (following evil norms). To think of conscience in this way as the judge of past action is to be on the verge of thinking of it also as the guide of future action. And though this latter aspect is not developed in the New Testament as part of the meaning of conscience, the duty to live by norms revealed by God is clearly affirmed in the teaching of Jesus and of his apostles. So, as the biblical doctrine of God as Triune (Father, Son and Holy Spirit) was developed into the Church doctrine of the Holy Trinity (see the Nicene and Athanasian Creeds), so the biblical doctrine of conscience was developed into the Church doctrine of the conscience. In each case the development is from Scripture and in accord with the spirit and teaching of Scripture. And as the use of the Church doctrine of the Holy Trinity can be enlightening when used to understand Scripture in its many-sided presentation of the LORD, so the developed doctrine of conscience can help us to understand the general sweep of moral teaching and exhortation provided in the Bible.

One final word about Jesus. We believe that he was truly a man but was the eternal Son of God made man—in the words of St. John he is 'the Word made flesh'. As man he was tempted and tested but he never sinned. Even when faced with cruel death and great suffering he did not sin. So, although Jesus never used the word conscience in his teaching, we can say that he always had a good conscience, for he lived in perfect communion with the Father and always did the Father's will. However, in his teaching he showed that he knew all about sin, guilt, and forgiveness, and of the need for disciples of the kingdom to have the right ideals and values by which to guide their lives.

4

Guilt, Forgiveness and Acceptance

A lot has been said and written in recent years about guilt. Confidential confessions of guilt from the couch or the comfortable chair have been numerous and varied. Popular magazines and newspapers have provided the confessions of guilt from the rich, famous and immoral for all to gloat over. Yet God, the living God, is rarely mentioned in such confessions of guilt.

But what is guilt? Like the word 'love' the word 'guilt' seems to be used in so many ways, pointing to a variety of feelings, convictions, anxieties and assumptions. Let us note a few of these so that we know what we are talking about when we talk of guilt before God—moral guilt which is offensive to his holy and righteous nature and contrary to his holy law.

FORMS OF GUILT

We are all familiar with *civil guilt*. If any court of law finds that you have broken the law, then you are judged guilty. It may be for a minor or major offence. Often civil guilt implies moral guilt (e.g. robbery and murder are usually immoral deeds); but, it need not always be the case that civil guilt is moral guilt. In some circumstances it will be necessary to disobey the State in order to obey God. This type of behavior was necessary in Nazi Germany and is necessary in certain countries today—only rarely perhaps in western democracies.

Most of us have experienced in large or small measure what may be called *psychological guilt*. In the jargon of Freudian psychotherapy this is the subjective experience of being internally condemned by one's super-ego. For example, a housewife and mother may have been brought up in a home where her mother was fastidious in her cleaning of the house and was scrupulous in preparing daily, at the same time, a full, cooked meal for the men of the family. She feels terribly guilty because she cannot either keep her house as clean as her mother's or cook as regularly or as well as her mother did. Normally, this kind of guilt is not moral and is not connected with the conscience—in the definition of conscience we are using.

Again, in the jargon, there is *existential ego guilt*. This refers to the sense of guilt that arises in you when you know and feel that you have not fulfilled one or another of the demands of the various human relationships you have in your life—e.g. as a father, a mother, a son, an employee, a church member, and so on. This is usually moral guilt (if your conscience is rightly judging) for it is a failure to love your neighbor as yourself and to do unto others as you would desire that they do unto you. To feel this kind of guilt, it is not necessary, however, to feel that you have also offended God. Only in the tender, mature Christian conscience will the feeling of having sinned against a fellow human being be intimately connected with sin against God, as the Father of all men.

Finally, there is *ontological guilt*. This is not the pain that arises from failure to relate decently and properly to other people. It is a sense of guilt for not being what you know you ought to be as a human person. It can be a feeling of alienation from the Cosmos, of being unfulfilled or of not facing your destiny. For the person who believes in the living God, Creator and Judge, it is a feeling of not being in a right relationship with him, of not being able to pray meaningfully to him as Father. Such a sense of guilt is moral guilt for it represents the recognition of failure to know God and to love him with the heart, soul, mind and strength.

GUILT AND GOSPEL

The Gospel of God concerning Jesus Christ exists because God is love and human beings are sinners. There is good news from heaven because we are in need of help. The moral guilt of every person before God is, from the standpoint of the Gospel, an objective fact. The law of the Lord and the Gospel are preached in order to call the hearer to recognize subjectively what is true objectively of all mankind—that it is sinful and falls short of God's glory. The good news of the kingdom of God (= God's kingly, fatherly and saving rule in Jesus Christ) calls the sinner to acknowledge his guilt before God, to reject the sin which produced guilt, and to receive forgiveness (= the cancellation of the guilt or debt of sin). If you have time look up Acts 2:38; 5:31; 10:43; 13:38; 26:18.

There is a world of difference between my having, on the one hand, a vague sense of being a guilty sinner before God—because I recognize as a fact that I have not kept the Ten Commandments—and, on the other, having what may be called an *awakened,* guilty conscience. It is possible as a Christian to have a *sleepy,* vaguely guilty conscience before God, because you have never felt the full impact of being awakened to the truth about God's character and to the enormity of personal sin against him. It is only as the Holy Spirit, who secretly and invisibly accompanies the preaching of the Gospel in the world, opens the door of your heart (to enlighten the mind and jolt/prick the conscience) that a real sense of personal guilt and shame arise.

Here is what Jesus said about the work of the Holy Spirit in his particular task of accompanying, as the invisible but real wind of God, the proclamation of the good news in the world:

> When the Holy Spirit comes, he will convince the world of sin and of righteousness and of judgment: of sin, because they do not believe in me; of righteousness, because I go to the Father and you will see me no more; of judgment because the prince of this world is judged (John 16:8–11).

Let us explore this teaching.

The Holy Spirit, who comes to the world from the Father in the name of the Incarnate Son (Jesus Christ, the exalted Lord), acts as a prosecutor amongst the people of the world. He prosecutes in such a way as to make a person recognize that he is truly guilty at God's bar, and in his conscience to feel guilty that he has not met God's standards and is not on his side. This internal prosecution occurs as the Gospel is heard with the ears, or read with eyes or seen (in demonstrations of Christian love in action) in the changed lives of believers. The process of prosecution may be long or short and the person being prosecuted will probably only be aware of feeling guilty, not specially aware of the of the presence of the Holy Spirit.

But guilty of what? Three areas are indicated by Jesus.

1. *Sin, expressed particularly and significantly as unbelief.* The Holy Spirit as prosecutor often causes a person to acknowledge that he is guilty of offending the Lord by having continually broken his moral law (expressed, for example, in the Ten Commandments and Sermon on the Mount). This is not usually experienced as a diffused sense of guilt with reference to all God's commandments but with reference to one or two specific commands—e.g. not to steal or not to bear false witness. However, the clearest indication of sin is the refusal to believe readily and immediately in the Lord Jesus and to receive him as Saviour and Lord—as the One who entered our space and time to save us from our sins. It is this unbelief, this self-assertion, which refuses to acknowledge Jesus as Saviour and which refuses to recognize a human being for what he is before God, the Judge, a sinner that is unmasked. The Holy Spirit prosecutes at this point, the point to which all disobedience of moral law and all selfishness point—*unbelief.*

2. *Righteousness, the vindication of Jesus as Messiah and Lord by his resurrection and ascension into heaven.* In prosecuting a person the Holy Spirit causes him to recognize that the only righteousness which is acceptable to God is that of Jesus, the Righteous One, who perfectly obeyed the will of God in his life. In comparison with his life, and in the mirror of the holy law of God, each and every person is guilty of unrighteousness. So the Holy Spirit prosecutes the hearers of the Gospel to make them see their unrighteousness and their need to participate in, or to be reckoned to possess, the righteousness of Jesus, the Representative and Substitutionary Man. This is why St. Paul's doctrine of justification by faith (= union with Christ, the Righteous One in faith) is such an important message for the guilty conscience to hear and to receive. However, until the prosecution has finished its task, there is no real appreciation of justification by faith.

3. *Judgment, the defeat of Satan, 'prince of this world', at the Cross and in Resurrection.* The Holy Spirit continues his prosecution by revealing what is the true position of Satan, the ruler of this world. To be a sinner and to be unrighteous is to be (whether recognized or not) in the employment of Satan, doing his will in the world. At the Cross and in the Resurrection, Satan was both judged and overcome. As Jesus was nailed to the Cross, Satan thought he had achieved a cataclysmic victory; but what he believed to be his victory was in fact

his judgment. He was shown to be what he is—the enemy of God and the enemy of the salvation of sinners. When Jesus broke the bonds of death and rose bodily from the grave, the great and permanent victory was achieved. The war is not yet over—the end will be at the close of the age—but Satan and his hosts are fighting a losing battle for they know they are losers. The Holy Spirit prosecutes in such a way as to convince people that as sinners without Christ they are on Satan's side, which is the losing side in the spiritual war that is being fought in the world.

We may say then that the Holy Spirit prosecutes with the aim of causing a sinner to feel ontological and moral guilt. And since the Spirit comes and works in the name of Jesus, it is his purpose so to prosecute that the cry, 'I am guilty, O God, be merciful to me a sinner' arises in the heart and there is a reaching out to ask, 'What must I do to receive forgiveness?'

(Perhaps it needs to be made clear that the person who is under conviction of sin through the internal work of the Holy Spirit will not necessarily explain how he feels with theological accuracy or even in the terms used above. What really matters at this stage is that the person with the awakened guilty conscience turns to God in the name of Jesus Christ, to repent of his sin and to believe the Gospel.)

The sane route to take is the route of repentance toward God and faith in the Lord Jesus. But people under conviction of sin, do not always act rationally or sensibly. They take the false route of the repression of the sense of guilt, and this leads to one of several spiritual maladies—depression, self-justification, or even aggressive tendencies. Sadly there are many who take this false route into their own sinful hearts, rather than the true route from their sins into the ocean of God's love and faithfulness.

FORGIVENESS, ACCEPTANCE AND JUSTIFICATION

What God offers and provides in the name of Jesus Christ is forgiveness of the guilt of sin. As St. Paul put it: 'In Christ we have redemption, the forgiveness of sins' (Col 1:14). What God does through Christ is to accept the guilty sinner as his adopted child and place his Spirit permanently within his heart. Again, as St. Paul expressed it: 'God has sent the Spirit of his Son into our hearts, crying "Abba, Father"' (Gal 4:6). What God declares in his heavenly court is that because of Christ, the Mediator, he places the sinner in a right relationship with himself, reckoning him to be righteous because united to Christ, the Righteous One. To quote St. Paul again: 'Since we are justified by faith, we have peace with God' (Rom 5:1).

As a result of this gracious work of God, the burden of guilt is removed (cleansed by the sacrifical blood of Christ) and the conscience is given a new start, as if it were a new creation. From now on, it cannot accuse the Christian believer of unbelief—for he is truly a believer in God through Jesus Christ; it cannot accuse him of not being in a right relationship with God, his Creator and Judge, for he is united to Christ, the Righteous One: and it cannot accuse him of belonging to the empire of Satan for he is a citizen of the kingdom of God and of Christ. In terms of all these things he has a clear conscience. And he sees his baptism as the outward and visible sign of his new relationship with God in Jesus Christ. St. Peter expressed it in this way: 'Baptism, which corresponds to this [safety in Noah's ark in the flood], now saves you, not as a removal of dirt from the body, but as an appeal to God for a clear conscience, through the resurrection of Jesus Christ' (1 Peter 3:21). This is why there is great emphasis in the New Testament on the freedom of a Christian—set free from all restrictions in order to be able joyfully and steadfastly to serve the Lord (we shall return to this theme in chapter 10).

Though the conscience of the Christian ceases to condemn him as an unbeliever, as without Christ and an enemy of God (how can it when it is known that 'there is no condemnation for those who are in Christ Jesus, Rom 8:1 ?), it continues to function as the judge and examiner of past action and the guide of future action. But this continuing role as judge and guide is no longer merely in the context of sin but it is in the context of grace where there is a genuine love for and delight in the law of the Lord. Yet this genuine love for God and his ways has to be educated by being taught from Scripture what is the way of life that God loves and approves. Thus the formation of the Christian conscience cannot be ignored. To ignore the need for growth into knowledge of God's revealed will is to face the possibility of easily backsliding into the old ways again.

The Christian never ceases to be a sinner in daily life and therefore he never ceases to be made aware of his sins and feel the need to confess them to the Lord, looking to Jesus Christ for absolution and forgiveness. He is like a child that has been legally adopted and therefore has a new name but retains the blood group and features inherited from his natural parents. A Christian has a new name, a new home, new prospects, new life and new relationships, but he has not lost his human body and his personality and his human nature. It is not that he intends to sin against God; but, he discovers that his sinful nature is a powerful reality and expresses itself in his words, attitudes and deeds when he least expects it and in ways that sometimes surprise him. So he continues to know guilt and to ask humbly for pardon. However, he asks for pardon as a child of the family, not as the child of an enemy. For Christ's sake this is granted and the conscience is clear again. His aim is a good conscience that finds little to condemn in his life.

When we referred above to 'existential ego guilt' we recognized that this often constitutes moral guilt, in that it is there because God's law has been broken. God's forgiveness in Christ covers all such guilt. This does not mean or imply, however, that in some instances there is not the moral requirement that a person who has wronged another (and who looks to God for forgiveness) should not go and put things right with that offended person. It is not possible to worship God in spirit and in truth if one is knowingly in a state of enmity with another person and one has not tried to bring reconciliation (see Matt 5:23-6). Since we use the Lord's Prayer often, it should not be easy to forget that we actually pray: 'Forgive us our sins as we forgive those who sin against us'. Those who are reconciled to God in and through Jesus Christ and who know that their sins are canceled, should find a desire within their hearts to live in peace and harmony with all men, especially those of the household of faith.

PSYCHOLOGICAL AND SOCIAL GUILT

Where there is serious psychological guilt it is advisable that the sufferer consult an experienced pastor or professional Christian therapist. For those with minimal psychological guilt, the message and power of the Gospel should be sufficient to bring freedom. To know and feel that one is accepted by God for Christ's sake, that one is called a child of God, that one is given the gift of the indwelling Spirit, and that one is a new creation, together with the experience of fellowship, worship and teaching in the local church, should be sufficient to bring wonderful release from such burdens. Release and freedom may not come in one moment but they will come sooner rather than later.

Social guilt is not a simple thing to deal with for it may be one of several things. It can be a manifestation of psychological guilt. Or it can be an aspect of moral guilt (e.g. feeling guilty for not being more generous in helping the poor and deprived in the city). Or, it can be part of that pain which all sensitive souls feel. I refer to the pain of empathy with the suffering and deprivation of fellow human beings. There is a sense in which I cannot be truly happy in this world until everyone else in this world is truly happy. Did not Jesus weep over Jerusalem and say that he would love to be able to embrace all its people?

I close this chapter with a quotation from Henri J. Nouwen, a writer on spirituality who has much emphasized the work of God as the healer of our memories. This healing of memory covers all kinds and types of pain and guilt for it is the deep work of God within our hearts and minds.

> By lifting our painful, forgotten memories out of the egocentric, individualistic, private sphere, Jesus Christ heals our pains. He connects them with the pain of all humanity, a pain he took upon himself and transformed. To heal, then, does not primarily mean to take pains away but to reveal that our pains are part of a greater pain, that our sorrows are part of a greater sorrow, that our experience is part of the great experience of him who said, 'But was it not ordained that the Christ should suffer and so enter into the glory of God' (cf. Luke 24:26). (*The Living Reminder,* 1977, p. 25.)

Nouwen goes on to state that hiding parts of our story, not only from our own consciousness but also (if we can) from God's eye, we claim a divine role for ourselves; we become judges of our own past and limit mercy to our own fears. If we do this we disconnect ourselves not only from our own suffering but also from God's suffering for us. Whatever our guilt, Jesus Christ, in the last analysis, is the only one who can *really* help.

5

Educating the Conscience

Here we come to the heart of the matter as far as the role of conscience as guide is concerned. The formation or education of conscience in the family, church and society may be looked at in terms of (a) the development of conscience in childhood, and (b) the education of conscience as a continuing process through life. This book is addressed to people of sixteen years and above and is, therefore, primarily about (b). However, since many adults are involved with children, as parents and teachers, it seems appropriate to make some comments on (a). But, before this is done, some general points need to be made which apply both to (a) and (b). In chapter 7 we shall concentrate on (b).

GENERAL PRINCIPLES

First of all, it must be recognized that the formation of conscience will, in certain important respects, be a process which for Christians will be distinctively different to that of their non-Christian friends, colleagues and relatives. This is because both children and adults are to be taught what is pleasing to God and what is condemned and disapproved by God. This point takes us back to the contents of chapter 2 where the question, 'Who am I?' was raised and answered. Not only is there secularist humanism in the air we breathe and in the spectacles by which we view the world, but we also have to face the impact of secularist humanism within the churches.

As long ago as 1955, Will Herberg wrote that: 'In the United States explicit secularism—hostility or demonstrative indifference to religion—is a minor or diminishing force; the secularism that permeates the American consciousness is to be found within the churches themselves and is expressed through men and women who are sincerely devoted to religion' (*Protestant-Catholic-Jew*, 1960 ed., p. 271). Things are not quite the same in the 1980s for explicit secularism is no longer a minor force. However, it still remains true that secularist thinking, dressed in religious terminology, is found in the churches in all kinds of ways—from the cult of materialism to the acceptance of abortion-on-demand. In morals it is seen, for example, in the adoption of what are called situation ethics and the demise of the traditional Christian view of conscience.

Situation ethics covers all views which reject the idea that the way to decide what is right and wrong (and thus to decide what to do) is always to apply rules (e.g. Ten Commandments). This approach accepts that such rules may throw helpful light on a situation and how to act in it but refuses to accept that the rules are prescriptive. In each situation one must be guided by love and the only kind of immorality that exists is the failure to love. One cannot say what ought to be done in the abstract; one must be in a situation and do what love requires to be done. This approach comes in sophisticated forms and the inexperienced and untutored can so easily be taken in by it. Love is a vague word and needs content, and the right content is that which Jesus and the apostles tell us that God approves. Paul Ramsey put his finger on the truth when he said of situation ethics as an approach that it is a 'prejudice in favor of individualist freedom, normlessness, traditional contemporaneity, and modern technical reason' (*The Situation Ethics Debate*, ed. Harvey Cox, 1968, p. 202). In other words it is secularist thinking in religious dress.

Perhaps the best way to illustrate the demise of the concept of conscience in the churches is to say that it is so often presented as 'my right to do what I think is right, for which I should not have to face the consequences'. This applies to those who openly deny the teaching of the denomination to which they belong and believe that if they are disciplined they are being cruelly or unjustly treated. It also applies in matters of rules. Take the case of the Anglican bishop (to whom priests in his diocese take an oath or promise of obedience) who told the rector of a city parish in his diocese that he must not allow irregularly ordained women priests to preside at holy communion in his parish. Then, contrary to all normal episcopal direction, he added that if the rector was compelled by his own conscience to allow one of these women to preside at the parish Eucharist, then he, the bishop (who possesses the authority over the parish) would have to respect and honor the rector's conscience. Such thinking and advice is muddled! To honor conscience requires that negative consequences are entailed—e.g. suspension as rector of the parish!

Secondly, when we talk about the formation of conscience, we are not thinking of a process of leading out of each person values and attitudes that are deeply embedded in the heart and mind, needing only to be given space in which to function. Certainly, being 'made in the image of God', each person has a basic moral awareness and also usually a basic desire to help other people. Yet human beings also suffer from the sickness of sin, the illness of gone-wrong-ness, and the malady of pride and selfishness. In them is a mixture of good and bad. It was Jesus who told his disciples that it is not 'unclean' food going into the stomach that defiles a human being; rather, it is what is already there in the heart that defiles. 'For from within, out of the heart of man, comes evil thoughts, fornication, theft, murder, adultery, coveting...' (Mark 7:21). Not that every person has always such thoughts and intentions in his heart all the time, but that each person has all the time some evil thoughts and intentions in his heart (which may be disguised as good, acceptable or reasonable feelings).

To form and educate the conscience is to enable a person to be encountered by God, in the name of Jesus Christ and in the power of the Holy Spirit. It is to receive what God has revealed of his will for mankind and to find that revelation recorded in the Bible. God made known his will to Moses, the prophets and apostles; in Jesus of Nazareth he provided the perfect example of a life arising from an educated conscience and obedient heart and will. To have an educated conscience is to have received and understood by the illumination of the Holy Spirit what God has revealed concerning human life, its moral and spiritual nature and purpose. The person who has an educated conscience will be able to say with the psalmist:

> The law of the LORD is perfect,
>   reviving the soul;
> the testimony of the LORD is sure,

> making wise the simple;
> the precepts of the LORD are right,
> rejoicing the heart;
> the commandment of the LORD is pure,
> enlightening the eyes;
> the fear of the LORD is clean,
> enduring for ever;
> the ordinances of the LORD are true,
> and righteous altogether.
> More to be desired are they than gold,
> even much fine gold;
> sweeter also than honey
> and drippings of the honeycomb (Ps 19:7–10).

The true Christian not only knows what is right but has a desire to do what is right.

Thirdly, the formation and education of the conscience is not achieved merely by the receiving or learning of material from the Bible. I may have much bible knowledge and not have an educated conscience. I have to be taught how to read the Bible in a discriminating way and how to recognize the principles of conduct that are presented therein. Then I need help with the art of applying them to my life and situation. In this sense, the word of God enters the heart more efficiently and deeply when it is intimately associated with Christian attitudes and actions. Too often it has been, 'Do as I say and not as I do'. Obviously a Christian family and a local church, where the word of God is believed, taught and obeyed, provide the natural ethos and opportunities for the education of conscience. And, of course, it is in the total context of society (of which family and church are parts) that problems, questions, and dilemmas arise which conscience must face.

Fourthly we need to recognize that only a combination of great ideas with good habits will produce mature and well-balanced characters. Great ideas without practical expression remain delights of the mind. Good habits alone become merely mechanical acts. In the committed Christian life there is need for great ideas and good habits. One without the other leads either to laxity (could-not-careless attitude) and on the other to legalism (must-keep-the-rules-at-all-costs).

Where are the great ideas? They are embedded and provided in the Gospel of our Lord Jesus Christ. This good news has many aspects to it—like a many-sided precious diamond. Likewise the apostolic teaching given to those who received the Gospel has many aspects to it—like the seven colors of the rainbow. We can only gain these great ideas by constant reading and meditation upon the contents of the Scriptures in the attitude of prayer and submissiveness to God as Lord. The use of devotional material, biographies of the saints and other Christian literature may also help. These ideas seem at their most meaningful when we engage in worship be it in public service or in lonely isolation before the holy Lord.

Ideas are intended in the divine scheme of things to be the source of, and inspiration for, Christian discipline. Ideas find practical expression and realization through habits. But what kind of habits? The traditional ones must be mentioned first for they cannot be avoided and they are the foundation of other habits. Regular attendance at worship each Lord's Day; humble reception of the sacrament of the Lord's Supper; time each day for meditation and prayer; fasting from time to time in order to keep the body under control and open the heart to God; almsgiving in a planned and sacrificial way; family prayers where applicable; and a host of other things.

A good habit has at least three characteristics. First of all it saves time; there is no need to waste time asking what to do if a habit has been formed—e.g. going to worship each Lord's Day. Secondly, it allows the mind to concentrate on the heart of the matter since the activity is familiar—e.g. on the content of the meaning of the liturgy in worship. And thirdly, a habit helps you to resist temptation because you are familiar with the right way and so it is not so hard to walk in that which is well known.

Ideas and habits belong together. The present generation is in danger of neither developing great (moral/spiritual) ideas nor creating good habits. There is too much emphasis on the failure (or apparent failure) of earlier generations and not enough recognition that the ideas from the Gospel do not lead to sterility but to fertility.

MORAL DEVELOPMENT

I once preached a sermon in a small, English medieval church and said something like this: 'We are not born with a conscience: it is formed and informed as we grow up.' A devout, intelligent lady commented afterward that she believed that each baby is born with a conscience, that is with the ability to judge between what is right and wrong. Each of us was partially right. Being made in the image of God, an infant possesses in potential or undeveloped form those features and characteristics which an adult, who is mature, possesses —a soul/spirit that is sensitive to God, the ability to think and reason, to make decisions and to exercise free choice. It may be said that each of us is born with the structure of a conscience but that this grows and is filled with content as we develop as human beings. In fact, in recent decades pyschologists and behavioral scientists in general have carefully studied the emotional, intellectual and moral development of human beings from infancy to adulthood.

To claim that the rudiments or structure of conscience is there from the beginning and functions with a content and in a manner which reflects the emotional, mental and moral growth of the child is a Christian claim. We must say something like this if we are to allow that the Holy Spirit can regenerate an infant, (e.g. before, during or just after infant baptism) and if we believe that a small child can have genuine religious experience—a sense of the presence of God and of the love of Jesus.

Having made such a claim there is every reason why we should turn to the work of researchers in the field of human growth and development for insight concerning the usual way in which growth occurs. From researchers who have worked in the areas pioneered by Sigmund Freud, we have theories as to the role of instinct and emotions in human development from infancy to adult life. Here the significant work of Erik Erikson could be mentioned—e.g. in his *Childhood and Society* and *Identity: Youth and Crisis.* Then, from researchers following in the footsteps of Jean Piaget we have theories of the cognitive, intellectual and moral development of children. Here the work of Lawrence Kohlberg has been very influential amongst educators—see his article on 'Moral Development' in the *International Encyclopedia of the Social Sciences* (1968) Volume 10. These two types of theory are developmental and are based on a model that is most easily conveyed by the illustration of the escalator. Each child is seen as passing through a sequence of phases, with each phase having its own features and characteristics and serving as a foundation for the next. Maturity is then defined in terms of the successful negotiation of, or passing through, each stage and as involving progressive mastery and integration. Immaturity is the possession of behavior patterns which are appropriate for an earlier stage of development than the chronological age of the child, youth, or adult.

The ability of a child to make evaluations from within, in contrast merely to responding to external requirement of the home, appears between the ages of four and six. This means that the values and standards of authority (e.g. parents) are taken in, are internalized and become the standards of the child, so that they influence his activity in the absence of the parents. However, from this period onward the child also comes under the influence of other children (the peer group) and values and standards are assimilated from this source as well. All parents know the problems of explaining or insisting on their standards when these clash with those of the peer group. Then, in later adolescence there are further developments.

Apart from developmental theories, there is the behaviorist approach (associated in the public mind with names like B. F. Skinner and H. J. Eysenck) which works on the general theory that all behavior is either facilitated or reinforced or discouraged and eliminated in relation to its consequences. No stages of development are associated with this approach and it is not concerned with feelings or intellectual growth. Rather it describes what happens in practice. Thus, from the perspective of learning theory, the contents of conscience are the result of the accumulation of conditioned responses which have been learned. So, for example, this approach points to the limitation of the effectiveness of punishment as a way of maintaining and enforcing standards unless there is an affectionate bond between those who administer and those who receive the punishment.

We look to psychologists to give us accurate descriptions of human growth and development, reaction and response, which are based on scientific observation and testing. We also look to wise Christians, with the right professional qualifications and experience, to interpret for the Church the findings of the behavioral sciences. Only in this way shall we benefit in our Christian education in home and church and school.

Amongst Christian educators great interest has been shown in the theories of Piaget and Kohlberg in cognitive and moral development and they have been used in Christian Education schemes. However, cognitive growth takes place not independently from but concurrently with emotional development, and the latter cannot be ignored or forgotten. So amongst Christian educators today there is the recognition and attempt to form approaches to moral education which are based on both these areas of human experience. And even when this is done there is need to look at the whole in the light of God's revelation in Christ. (This is what Paul J. Philibert attempts to do in his 'Conscience: Developmental Perspectives from Rogers to Kohlberg' in *Horizons* (the journal of the College Theology Society) 1979, 6/1). From a Christian perspective, it is very important that (1) the whole context in which growth (physical, mental, moral, emotional and spiritual) occurs, and (2) the nature and type of morality which is conveyed to children, be right and wholesome. Mistakes made in the education of the conscience of a child are not easily undone.

This is not the place to discuss theories from the behavioral sciences. There is usually at least one person in each large church who is familiar with such theories and can explain them to parents and teachers. What is needed here is practical advice. So what follows are various comments intended to promote serious thought on the education of conscience in childhood and adolescence.

1. Children need to be exposed to Christian worship from their earliest days. The ethos and exhilaration of worship, the atmosphere of reverence, the sense of the numinous, and the life-giving presence of the Holy Spirit who comes in the name of, and with the virtues of, the exalted Lord Jesus are felt in our spirits whatever be our age. To keep infants and children out of worship until they are judged old enough to understand is a mistake. Baptized infants belong to the family of God, especially when that family engages in its most ennobling activity, worship of Almighty God. In and through worship the conscience is kept in contact with the living Lord.

2. All who teach children Christian morality should live by that morality. Conscience grows more quickly toward Christ when it is influenced by both word and action (that exemplifies the word). One writer has expressed it in this way:

> Probably the most devastating type of parental behavior for children's moral development is that which deliberately and openly flouts the moral principles which parents verbalize and try to instill in their children. The 'white lies' parents tell, or ask children to tell for them, and the frequent forgotten or broken promises can do more to undermine a child's trust than preaching or religious education can counteract. [Dorothea McCarthy, 'The Development of Normal Conscience' in *Con-*

science: Its Freedom and Limitations, ed. W.C.Bier S.J., 1971, pp.39–61]

It is so often the case that parents complain about the immorality of their teenage children when they have not provided them with a good example.

3. A distinction must be made in the way we educate the conscience of the young child (up to 5 or 6) and the older child. In the earliest stages children have to be told what is right and wrong with loving firmness and authority and they must be made to behave accordingly. You do not reason with a four-year old as though he were a college student! On the other side, you are careful, for example, not to call a child of this age a liar, for the difference between fact and fiction, reality and fantasy is blurred at this stage of growth.

Older children demand and need explanations of what is right and wrong but they still need a firm but loving hand to cause them to do what they are told to do. It is right to tell an eight-year old that he must seek to love his neighbor as he loves himself and to do unto other children what he would like them to do to him. It is also right and necessary that he be helped in practice to work out what this means in terms of the life and relations of an eight year old! Further, in making judgments as to whether or not such a child has done what he has been taught to do, allowance needs to be made both for the emotional stage at which he is, and whether he is able intellectually to see all the issues that the adult can see.

Rather than criticizing each other for the way in which they bring up children, Christian parents need to get together in order to help each other in this noble but demanding task.

4. Since the influence of peer groups is so important (and since the pressure to conform from advertising and the media is so persuasive) parents need to do all they can to help their children become committed members of viable Christian youth organizations or groups. Indeed, some parents choose to attend one church rather than another because it offers a variety of activities for young people. Hopefully such youth groups help to show the viability and the superiority of the Christian moral way in today's world. Adolescents and teenagers are going through a period of adjustment and growth and need to have parents and pastors who are available, wise and understanding.

5. Morality should never be taught as an independent area of life

which is unconnected with the rest of life. Morality is intimately connected with personal existence, integrity and responsibility. It cannot be prized apart from Christian faith and faithfulness. It is an aspect of Christian discipleship. The way you live and your motivation is under Jesus Christ, your Lord.

6. A distinction needs to be made, as soon as children can understand it, between what is right and wrong in terms of culture, good manners, school rules and family traditions, on the one side, and, on the other, the content and the application of God's holy and moral law. This distinction will be the easier to explain if the children are in a school where they have good teaching in history, geography and related subjects, for they will see how people dress, eat, socialize, live in community and are politically organized in different societies and cultures. Far too often Westerners have confused God's commandments with their specific cultural norms in their commendation of the Gospel to other parts of God's world. It helps to let children know very early in life that Jesus was a Jew, living in (by modern standards) a backward country, and with a complexion that was probably more olive than pinky white.

7. Maturing adolescents should be taught that they are personally responsible for their lives, their thoughts and actions and for the moral choices they make. God has given them the ability to think and to choose and also the will to put into action what they believe they should do. Of course they need help in making moral choices and they need to realize that to do what is right may have consequences that are not pleasant. And they need to be encouraged to see their personal responsibility as that which they exercise as they respond to God as he graciously offers them his help and salvation in the name of Jesus Christ, the Lord.

Other points could be made. In discussion with friends you will be able to add to these and perhaps modify the above seven points.

6

The Formation of Conscience

An educated or mature Christian conscience does not come simply as the result of being born again of the Spirit, or making a decision for Christ at an evangelistic crusade, or being baptized in the Triune Name, or becoming a church member. It is not infused into your heart as blood is transfused into your body when you are anaemic. It does not happen overnight or in a week.

SLOW BUT SURE PROGRESS

Having entered the family of God, you have to grow into Christ in love and wisdom; having enrolled in the school of Christ you have to learn what is taught there; and having entered the kingdom of Christ you have to submit to the King and his laws. In fact, your conscience is educated as, in union with Jesus Christ through the Holy Spirit, the mind of Christ is formed within you and you learn to act according to that mind. In principle, all that is in the mind of Christ is yours now for he is your Saviour and your Lord; but, it takes time and spiritual discipline for you to receive what he has to share with you and for you to learn how to put it into practice. As you confess that Jesus Christ is your Lord, as well as Lord of the Church and universe, and as you find out what that confession means in a sinful world, so the mind of Christ is formed within you.

The formation of Christian conscience cannot occur in individualistic isolation. It is possible for me to call myself a Christian, read the Bible, pray and, by choice, not to attend the worship and fellowship of a Christian congregation. I can attempt to educate my own conscience; but, if I try to do so, what usually happens is that I gain an imbalanced conscience, which majors on minors and puts in first place what should go in second place. (We shall return to this theme in chapter 7).

To confess Jesus as Lord is to join others who confess him as Lord. Only in the fellowship, worship, warmth and witness of a local church can a Christian find the atmosphere and ethos in which his moral and spiritual consciousness can grow in a balanced manner. God calls each Christian to confess Jesus as Lord and to be taught and to discover what this confession means as he/she exercises membership in a church, which is the household of faith. Then, from that base, the confession of Jesus as Lord at home, work or leisure is more effective and meaningful.

Moral and spiritual growth occur only as what is known to be God's will is obeyed. It is no good wanting to know the whole body of Christian morality in one lesson. Certainly you need to be hungry for the word of God but it is only as you learn to live in the light of what you know that other parts of the Christian faith begin to make an impact and demand upon you. As you allow Christ the Lord to reign in your life, and as he shares his mind with you, you will discover more of his loving demands upon you as the days go by. Thus your conscience will be constantly guiding you into new areas where Christ is telling you he wants to reign as Lord. Your heart, mind and will are like a vast territory into which Christ has entered. He wants to rule the whole territory and you wish him to do so; but, you are in the strange position of only discovering gradually how he intends to exercise his rule.

Perhaps this example will help. Let us suppose that there is a family who live near to you and you know that they are on hard times. Your conscience tells you to help but it does not tell you any more. At this stage you can stifle conscience by thinking of other things or by giving yourself other tasks to do. But you choose to call upon the family, taking a copy of your church magazine or bulletin with you as a way of initiating conversation. You reach the house, get into conversation at the door, eventually are invited in and then you discover several ways in which you or your church can help this family. Christ the Lord has led you into this situation and now he calls your church to come and offer help. I leave it to your imagination as to what kinds of things the family needs and how this could be the way that God has ordained for this family to encounter God's love through you and your church.

Or take another example. Let us suppose that you are a married man and that you are having marital difficulties and not living with your wife. However, you are not legally separated and you are not thinking right now of divorce, for you hope that will both get over this crisis and resume family life. Being a man with a strong sexual drive, you have been having sexual intercourse with a girl from work who says she likes you. Then your conscience begins to speak loudly. Jesus the Lord says to you, 'You shall not commit adultery; fornication is a sin against heaven'. Then, you pray for help and you tell the girl that you must cease this relationship; and you seem to be able to pray again, and you feel that somehow God still loves you. But sometimes when you see this girl you find a powerful lust within you causing you to wish to get into bed with her as soon as possible. You resist this but it is there. And it keeps returning and you try to dismiss it. One day you are reading the Sermon on the Mount and you find these words: 'You have heard that it was said, "You shall not commit adultery". But I say unto you that everyone who looks at a woman lustfully has already committed adultery with her in his heart.' This word teaches that God's law points deeply into you and you pray that God will forgive you and give you power to resist the temptation to lust.

The point in both these examples is that only as you take one step of obedience to conscience (= to Christ the Lord) can you effectively know what is the next. This is what the Christian continually experiences on a wide front in a variety of ways. It is not that the Christian advances in one straight line, by one thing leading to another. Rather it is that he is moving from a base line along many parallel lines and he has to make progress in each one of them.

THE NEED FOR BASICS

This is why there is need for new Christians to be given the basics of the moral way of life that Christ commands. A quick way into knowledge of this life is to learn the Ten Commandments—as they are interpreted in the New Testament—and to begin to work out (with the help of others) what they mean in practice. The Christian is to obey the Ten Commandments as Christian, not as a Jew or a

Muslim. Here is a rendering of them which sees them in the light of the New Testament and so in the light of Christ. It is part of an English Liturgy (Holy Communion Series 3).

The Commandments

Our Lord Jesus Christ said, If you love me, keep my commandments: happy are those who hear the word of God and keep it. Hear then these commandments which God has given to his people, and take them to heart. I am the Lord your God: you shall have no other gods but me.

1. You shall love the Lord your God with all your heart, with all your soul, with all your mind, and with all your strength.

2. You shall not make for yourself any idol. God is spirit, and those who worship him must worship in spirit and in truth.

3. You shall not dishonor the name of the Lord your God. You shall worship him with reverence and awe.

4. Remember the Lord's and keep it holy.
Christ is risen from the dead: set your minds on things that are above, not on things that are on earth.

5. Honor you father and mother.
Live as servants of God: honor all men: love the brotherhood.

6. You shall not commit murder.
Do not nurse anger against your brother: overcome evil with good.

7. You shall not commit adultery.
Know that your body is a temple of the Holy Spirit.

8. You shall not steal.
You shall work honestly and give to those in need.

9. You shall not be a false witness.
Let everyone speak the truth.

10. You shall not covet anything which belongs to your neighbor.

> Remember the words of the Lord Jesus: It is more blessed to give than to receive. Love your neighbor as yourself, for love is the fulfilling of the law.

Of course there are other ways of seeing the basic morality of the Law of Moses filled out by the teaching of Jesus and the apostles. The old catechisms of the Lutheran, Presbyterian and Anglican Churches do such a thing.

As you follow the direction of your conscience, which is formed by the commandments, you will find that you fail, both by deliberate choice (a sin of commission) and by oversight or ignorance (a sin of omission) completely to obey what you know is required of you by God's law fulfilled in Jesus Christ. This is where your conscience will accuse you and send you in penitence to God in the name of Jesus, your Saviour, to confess your sins and receive his assurance of pardon. 'If we say we have no sin we deceive ourselves and the truth is not in us. If we confess our sins, God is faithful and just and will forgive us our sins and cleanse us from all unrighteousness' (1 John 1:8-9). It is possible both to confess your sins privately in your daily devotions and in a service of public worship, where the word of pardon is pronounced to the penitent by the presiding minister. For your conscience to mature in its direction you must obey it both when it condemns (by confession of sins) and when it directs (by obedience).

PERSONAL GROWTH WITHIN CHRISTIAN FELLOWSHIP

The commandments are a start; but, in fact, you will always come back to them, seeing ever deeper demands in them. You will grow as you become more familiar with the contents of the Gospels and Epistles of the New Testament, as you hear sermons on them, as you read books about Christian duty, as you engage in discussion with fellow Christians about Christian morality today, as you encounter problems, questions and difficulties in your daily life and seek to resolve them in the light of your Christian commitment to Jesus Christ. Conscience matures as you grow into Christ and into his body, the church, and as you seek to obey him as Lord in his world. But this maturation is, as was emphasized earlier, not individualistic, achieved in isolation. It is certainly a personal maturation but it is experienced and achieved by the grace of God as you knowingly and unreservedly play your part in the life of your church. For most of us, maturation is not a smooth, evolutionary development of gradual growth in knowledge and obedience. Rather it is the experience of climbing mountains and falling into valleys and of crossing difficult rivers and wading through swamps. And it involves some hard, practical thinking, applying God's word to complex situations. Some people find it helpful to have a 'spiritual director' with whom they discuss their problems/questions of conscience. Others belong to small 'cell' groups where there is intimate sharing not only of problems of conscience but also of joys and sorrows.

Let us be clear. You are not like a computer which can be programmed with the right information and then invariably act in accordance with that information in all places at all times. Your heart and mind are not a kind of vacuum into which a right attitude and code of morality can be poured; your will is not like an automatic gear box which always responds according to a fixed ratio.

You are you, not an automaton. You have a unique personality. And you did not begin the Christian life with a heart from which all evil impulses have been taken away and a mind and will perfectly adjusted to the will of the Lord. You began your Christian life as a forgiven sinner whom God had accepted for Christ's sake. You remain a sinner and will remain so until your dying day. Certainly God loves you and has placed his Spirit within your heart. He views you in Christ as a new creation. Yet in reality, on earth, in day-to-day experience you belong to two worlds—to the world where Christ is, seated at God's right hand in glory, and to this world where there is sin and evil, suffering and shame, and where every human being is a sinner.

This is why in public worship Christians pray a prayer like this ancient collect for purity:
>Almighty God,
>to whom all hearts are open,
>all desires known,
>and from whom no secrets are hid:
>cleanse the thoughts of our hearts
>by the inspiration of your Holy Spirit,
>that we may perfectly love you,
>and worthily magnify your holy Name;
>through Christ our Lord.

And it is why they make confessions of sin: 'We have sinned against you, O God, in thought and word and deed'. It is also why they rejoice in their heavenly union with Jesus Christ, their exalted Saviour and Lord, and think or say such words as these: 'Accept, O God, through Christ, our great high priest, our sacrifice of thanks and praise . . .'

Your conscience matures as you grow not only in knowledge of what God requires of you but also in recognition of your own sinfulness and of your total dependence upon the Lord Jesus as Saviour. In a 'normal' Christian life within a 'normal' Christian church, these developments should occur simultaneously and harmoniously. It is impossible to be *wholly* aware of what Christ the Lord *totally* requires of you except on a day-to-day basis. When you have submitted to his rule today, and confessed your failures of today, then you will know what is right and wrong for tomorrow. To state this is not to deny that there are no fixed principles such as the Ten Commandments, the two great commandments to love God and the neighbor, and the command of Christ to love one another as he loves us. Rather it is to claim that the whole, moral demand of God in Christ has to be interpreted by me in my situation day by day. For example, to know 'You shall not bear false witness against your neighbor' is basic to Christian knowledge of right and wrong: however, in everyday life, as a disciple of Jesus and his obedient servant, you have to decide (as guided by his Spirit) when there is a point of moral decision where you have to choose to bear or not bear false witness. For many of us such a decision is a daily reality.

It is an obvious point but is well worth making. Individual Christians share the privilege of being children of God and the duty of obeying their heavenly Father. So, in terms of what they ought to be and to do, there is much in common between them. However, since each Christian has a particular position—e.g. a father, mother, son, daughter, brother or sister—and a particular job (a student, housewife, engineer or schoolteacher), it is required by the Lord that in these specific areas the Christian educates his conscience as to what is his duty. This education will be based on biblical principles but will include 'secular' knowledge as well—e.g. technical knowledge in the case of an engineer. Again, it is right and good for Christians with similar vocations and jobs to compare experiences and help each other.

The formation or education of conscience is, of course, an aspect of the total growth toward Christian maturity—'You must be perfect, as your heavenly Father is perfect' said Jesus (Matt 5:48), and Paul claimed:'I press on toward the goal for the prize of the upward call of God in Christ Jesus' and then added, 'Let those of you who are mature be thus minded' (Phil 3:14–15). There is no shortcut to the goal of perfection. The closer that Christians get to the goal the more they feel their sinfulness and unworthiness; yet, paradoxically, the more the Spirit within them testifies that they are truly and undoubtedly children of God (Gal 4:6; Rom 8: 15–16).

STANDARDS AND MOTIVES

Within the context of full participation in the worship, life and witness of the church, a productive way of thinking about the formation of conscience is to consider the standards and motives of the life that truly confesses Jesus as Lord. It is good to ask the basic question: What criteria are Christians to use to judge not merely what is right and wrong, but also when there are several possibilities of right, how to choose the best of these. There are two basic criteria to which the Bible points and Christian tradition confirms: they are (1) God loves certain types of action and hates other types, and (2) Your motive as well as your action must be right. (Dr. J. I. Packer explains these criteria in *Law, Morality and the Bible,* ed. B. N. Kaye, 1978, pp. 179ff.) Let us briefly examine them.

God loves certain types of action and hates other types. It is important in our permissive age for Christians to realize that God has already made his choice of what he loves and hates. So when he says, 'Be perfect as I am perfect' and 'Be holy as I am holy' he really means business. All through the Bible there are statements both of what God loves and approves and of what he hates and disapproves. The LORD loves justice and hates injustice: 'I, the LORD, love justice: I hate robbery and wrong' (Isaiah 61:8). The Lord loves righteousness and sincere spiritual worship: he hates hypocrisy, pretense and false worship. 'I hate, I despise your feasts and I take no delight in your solemn assemblies . . . Take away from me the noise of your songs: to the melody of your harps I will not listen. But let justice roll down like waters, and righteousness like an everflowing stream' (Amos 5:21–4). Further, the Lord hates teaching from within the churches which confuses Christian liberty (for which see chapter 10 below) with a license to do what you like, when you like. This heresy was found in churches of Asia Minor and so the Lord congratulated the church in Ephesus for its general rejection of the heresy: 'You hate the works of the Nicolaitans, which I also hate' (Rev 2:6). The Nicolaitans were the heretics whose heresy is often called anti-nomianism (against law).

What God loves and hates may also easily be deduced from what the Lord commands. If you carefully read the Ten Commandments, the two great commandments to love God and the neighbor and the specific command to love as Christ loves you, then you can quickly make a list of what God loves and hates, approves and condemns. For example, God loves to see genuine respect for human life, property, marriage and parents and he much approves truthfulness and honesty in everyday life, sincere worship and the setting of a day apart for that worship. And God hates such things as idolatry (an ancient and—please note—a modern phenomenon as H. Schlossberg, *Idols for Destruction,* 1983, points out), profanity, adultery, immorality, dishonesty, hatred and covetousness. In fact St. Paul provided on several occasions lists of things condemned by God (see e.g. Gal 5:19–21).

By carefully reading the New Testament within the fellowship of your church and in your home, you can easily compile lists of attitudes and activities which the Lord loves and hates, approves and condemns. Begin, for example, with the Sermon on the Mount and you will see how Jesus shows what kind of life a disciple of the kingdom should live, what virtues and values should guide his inner and outer life, and how he should perform the duties of prayer, almsgiving and fasting. Turn then to one of St. Paul's Letters, to the Ephesians for example, and take a section from there—e.g. 4:17–5:2. This section in the Letter begins with a reference to a typical pagan life-style (true of the majority in ancient times and so true of many in modern society also), notes how the consciences of pagans are dulled through constant sinning, shows what Christian conversion means, and then points out what the Lord approves and condemns.

As the Lord's messenger, Paul makes abundantly clear that the Lord hates such things as telling lies, uncontrolled anger, the ways of the devil, robbery and theft, dishonesty, harmful words, bitterness of spirit, passion, hateful feelings and insulting words and behavior. In contrast, the Lord loves all that is in, and proceeds from, the Lord Jesus, together with truthfulness, helpful words, good actions, kindness, tender-heartedness and genuine love.

When you know the Lord's will then you ask him to help you live in such a way that you do what he approves and do not do what he forbids. This means that you need to pray for yourself and fellow church members what Paul prayed for the members of the church in Philippi: 'I pray that your love will keep on growing more and more, together with true knowledge and perfect judgment, so that you will be able to choose what is best' (TEV, 1:9).

2. *Your motive as well as your action must be right.* God looks into your heart and he knows your thoughts, feelings, and motives better than you know them yourself. By placing his Spirit within your heart, he has also put his love within you: 'God's love has been poured into our hearts through the Holy Spirit, which has been given us' (Rom 5:5). And God looks for love, his love, as the basis of your relationship with himself and with people around you. This is made very clear in the 'hymn of love' provided by St. Paul in 1 Corinthians 13.

> Love is patient and kind; love is not jealous or boastful; it is not arrogant or rude. Love does not insist on its own way; it is not irritable or resentful; it does not rejoice at wrong, but rejoices in the right. Love bears all things, believes all things, hopes all things, endures all things.

And to underline this, God has made it clear that his own motivation in sending his Son into our dark and sinful world was love: 'God so loved the world that he gave his only-begotten Son . . .'

The way that love should operate as the basic motive of Christian behavior may be illustrated with reference to the role of a referee in a soccer match (North Americans are becoming more familiar with this game of soccer). The job of the referee is to apply the written rules of the game in such a way that the game flows smoothly and is enjoyed by the players and appreciated by the spectators. So the following may be said of a good referee:

1. He thoroughly learns the rule of the game and the way in which they are usually applied.

2. During the game he always seeks to be in the best position to see what is going on so that he can make a fair decision. This means that he must keep up with the game wherever it is on the big field and he must keep his eyes open to see incident off as well as on the ball.

3. When he is not sure of what actually happened, he will consult the linesmen (who run along the side of the field to indicate when the ball is out of play) However, he will not listen to shouts from the crowd telling him what to decide for he knows that people in the crowd want one side or the other to win and so are not objective in their judgments.

4. He will sometimes allow play to go on even when there has been an offense; he will do this because the side offended against has possession of the ball and can benefit from this possession. This is to play the advantage rule.

Now we can see how the role of the good referee provides an indication of how love functions as the basic motive of the Christian life.

1. Love, placed within you by God, leads you to want to know about him and his will. Love makes you consult the rule-book, the sacred Scriptures and the way that they have been understood in the life of the Church over the years. You want to know what God approves and loves and what he condemns and hates.

2. Love directs you to place yourself always in the best position from which to make a moral choice. This means that you have to keep your eyes wide open to what is happening in your society so that you are wise before rather than after the event. It also means that you need to be fully acquainted as far as it is possible with the consequences of one action or another. For example, the decision whether or not to invite an aged parent to come and live with you; and from the other way round, the decision whether or not to go and live with a son or daughter.

3. Love directs you to consult a fellow Christian (a wise one) when you are not clear what to do—just as the referee consults the linesman. When you are not sure what to do, do not listen to the voice of contemporary, secularist society for it is partisan (not on God's side).

4. Love will sometimes tell you to disregard your right to do something in order to submit to the requests of others. This is playing the advantage rule. St. Paul urged the strong Christians in the church at Corinth to play this rule by giving up their right to eat meat which had originally been offered as a sacrifice in a pagan temple. This was so that their action could be controlled by the principle of not offending the consciences of their weaker brethren and sisters, who believed that it was wrong to eat such meat. There

are plenty of modern parallels but I take one from the Church of England. This Church has two Prayer Books, an old one and a new one (1980). The rector of a parish has the right to decide which of these two is used for occasional services—baptisms, weddings and funerals. Let us suppose that a particular rector strongly favored the services in the new book. According to church law it is his right to use them. However, if he knows that his congregation for an occasional service will more appreciate for good reasons the old book than the new, he will wisely submit to their expressed desires.

A final comment. Too many Christians ask: What is the minimum I should be and do as a Christian to glorify God and serve his world? The New Testament tells us that we should ask: What is the most I should be and do to glorify God and serve his world? Our consciences need so to be formed that the second, rather than the first question, is the one we ask and seek to answer positively.

7

Training the Conscience

In the last two chapters our emphasis has been on the formation of the individual Christian conscience within the setting of family and church and based on the teaching of the sacred Scriptures. It is now necessary to widen the horizons of our thinking and thus of the education of the conscience by two further considerations. They are (1) the local congregation is a part of (or microcosm of) the one, holy, catholic and apostolic Church, and (2) the family and the church are parts of the larger society in which they are set.

CATHOLICITY AND LOYALTY

The situation of the Church of God in the world is not that of being a united body of people, who form one (and one only) congregation in each locality. The model of the Kentucky Fried Chicken or the MacDonald's Hamburger empires, with one selling point in each locality, does not convey the state of the Church in the world. The reality is more like the model of a cluster of chain stores—Woolco, Sears, K-Mart, etc.—each selling much the same types of goods and each in competition with the other. The Church is not a visible unity in the world: regrettably and sadly it is divided.

Certainly each local church that confesses the faith of the TRIUNE LORD and looks to the Bible for authoritative teaching on faith and morals is in spiritual union with the exalted Lord Jesus, Head of the whole Church. Yet since a local church is, at least to some degree, in competition with other local churches in the neighborhood the Christian has to face this fact. Also he has to face the implication that each local church usually belongs to a larger national or international denomination and that this means that it has certain distinctive emphases or origins which 'denominate' it (e.g. Anglicanism is from England, the land of the Anglo-Saxons). He may be a member of a local church by specific choice or conviction; on the other hand, he may attend because this has been the family church for years.

The committed Christian surely recognizes that membership of a specific church implies loyalty to that church—but not a blind loyalty. Further his moral reason tells him that his loyalty to Christ also requires him to recognize that there are other churches nearby which are just as worthy of the name of Christian as is his church. So we must say that the conscience of the mature Christian must be educated not only by the doctrinal and ethical traditions of his own denomination but also by similar traditions (e.g. of the Anglican, Presbyterian, Methodist, Lutheran, Baptist and Roman Catholic). Obviously it takes time to gain such an understanding but the main essentials of it can be gained from major reference books and through fraternal discussion and joint evangelistic and social activities with other churches. Loyalty to Jesus Christ, Head of the whole Church, requires this larger education of the conscience. And, among other benefits, it keeps you from bigotry and ignorant prejudice.

A tendency in modern society is to be loyal only to what you like in the period when you like it. This is part of the general emphasis on my rights with little accompanying emphasis on 'my duties'. Far too many splits (in both local churches and denominations) have been caused because of the combination of a lack of loyalty and a (mis-guided) emphasis on the rights of the individual conscience. So often it has been the case that a member of a church (or a minister of a denomination) becomes convinced that a particular teaching or rule is wrong, erroneous, heretical or sinful. This teaching, in its positive content or its negative criticism, becomes very prominent in his thinking and the more he thinks about it, the more he feels he must do something about it. The option of leaving the church and going quietly to another which is more in line with his sentiments is open, but he chooses instead to make a great issue of it and to take others with him. He works on the principle that when his (mis-guided) conscience says 'You must do this . . .' then this dictate applies to others as well. Now, were the spirit of loyalty stronger in his mind and heart, he would have been (1) less likely to have been so impressed by the new teaching and (2) more likely to have shared his concerns with others in a friendly, humble manner. Then, if he did finally feel the need to leave, he would not cause so much distress and division by his quiet departure.

On several campuses I have met seminarians who have told me that they have forsaken—on grounds of conscience—the historical denomination in which they have been baptized and nurtured to faith in Jesus. The reasons are always to do with the apparent lack of commitment to the teaching of the Scriptures or to what they call 'liberal' (= negatively radical) theology. In very few cases have these people seriously considered either the solid doctrinal tradition of the denomination they are forsaking or the possibility of renewal of that denomination by the word of God in the power of the Spirit. They go off to join new groups who have enthusiasm but no roots in history and they quote the example of Martin Luther, as though they had agonized as he did for years with a guilty conscience before God. Here again the spirit of individual rights and speedy answers (like instant food!) dominate the conscience and the old virtue of loyalty is not given a chance to inform the conscience. (See further 'Testing Claims' in chapter 8 below.)

Another related area which demands comment is that which used to be called 'private judgment' and is often mistakenly spoken of—by rigid Roman Catholics and earnest Protestants—as the distinctive doctrine of Protestantism. Private judgment may be expressed as follows: 'I have the right to decide the meaning of a part or the whole of Scripture as it relates to me in my relationship to God and as I follow Christ.' It is put forward in this way as the opposite of: 'The meaning of a part or the whole of Scripture as it relates to me in my relationship to God and as I follow Christ is decided by others' (others being an authority like the Pope). Both statements contain truth but neither contains the whole truth. One majors on the individualistic approach to conscience and the other majors on the quality of loyalty to those in authority.

I (or you) have the right to decide what Scripture means for me (you) when I (you) have diligently made use of all the available forms of help which assist the search for clarity of mind. These basic helps, which include the ancient creeds (Apostles', Nicene, Athanasian), lexicons, commentaries, Bible and theological dictionaries and other reference material point both to catholicity (they arise within the whole Church not in one denomination) and to loyalty (I use them because they are part of God's gifts to the whole Church). Now since to decide for yourself what the Bible means for today is more than a lifetime's task, you have to take on trust, in the spirit of loyalty for most of the time what you learn within your own church and what you learn about the Faith from other local churches (and Christian magazines etc.). In order that your conscience can function you must believe in your heart and mind in certain truths and be committed to a body of teaching. Therefore you cannot escape, if you are a responsible person, from the exercise of private judgment. But the exercise of private judgment as you grow in Christian maturity will be based on an ever growing experience of, and use of, catholicity (the material made available in the Church over the centuries which helps to convey the meaning of the Bible). In this sense, catholicity and loyalty belong together. Neither blind loyalty nor arrogant individualism is the answer. What is my right needs to be moulded by participation in catholicity and by my exercise of loyalty. My rights and my duties belong together.

SOCIAL AND POLITICAL RESPONSIBILITY

The education of my conscience by the revealed will of God so that I know how to behave in the basic relationships of my life—in family, at work and in church—has been emphasized in earlier chapters. But there is a further, related area where the education of the conscience is needed and that is my role as a citizen of a democratic society and of the human race in the whole world. In a democratic society I have the right and duty to vote as well as the right and duty to seek to influence general culture and to inform or change government policy through appropriate action. Too many Christians are content to sit back and be as little involved as possible in political and social thinking (and action) as long as things seem to be going their way. Reasons for such an attitude vary—from the belief that they should only get involved in evangelism to the more selfish feeling of 'I am all right and let things stay that way'. In recent years, some evangelicals (who are known for their commitment to evangelism) have felt that they ought to take their role as citizens seriously (see e.g. *Evangelism and Social Responsibility: An Evangelical Commitment* [the Grand Rapids Report of 1982], with a preface by

Dr. John Stott). We hope that those who selfishly turn a blind eye to their social responsibility will be pricked in their consciences to turn an open eye.

Those who are more active than others in social or political action are usually said to have a 'social' or a 'radical' conscience. By describing them in this manner we say that they feel a duty to be involved to bring about such changes as they think are necessary for human progress. Of people who have been imprisoned because their moral convictions caused them to break (unjust?) laws we refer to as 'prisoners of conscience'. The prison here is not their own thinking or feeling but a jail or a psychiatric hospital (in Russia), or their own home (house arrest in South Africa).

There is a real sense in which all Christian should have a 'social' and 'political' conscience. Why? Let us recall some basic Christian facts. They live in God's world. All human beings are God's creatures and he loves them. God longs to see justice in human affairs. Jesus Christ, the Just One, died to pardon the sins of the unjust—human beings of all kinds. Then Christians possess the democratic vote (the origin of which in western society is related to the general influence of Christianity in the culture) and they have the possibility of influencing society both individually and corporately as the body of Christ.

To possess an informed conscience on social and political matters is easier said than done. There is a bewildering complexity of information to absorb on most large issues and, to complicate the scene, it comes from sources (e.g. the media) which cannot claim to be infallible. (In contrast, the information of what God approves and disapproves in the Bible is infallible, even if our interpretation of it is fallible.) Because of the complexity, it may be that most of us have to rely on the judgment of those whom we deeply respect in order to come to judgments on such issues. To do this, however, does not mean we should not try to see what are the basic moral issues involved and ask how God's moral law applies to them and in them.

In judging these complex moral issues of our time (e.g. on whether to produce nuclear warheads, on relations with countries that have racist legislation or deny fundamental human rights, and on the right policy to adopt concerning welfare and education) people of sincere Christian commitment come to different conclusions! In some cases it is because one is better informed than the other or that one is more Christian in his thinking than the other. However, the most common reason is more complicated. It is that human beings, including Christian believers, are finite in their understanding and sinful in their natures. (We shall return to this theme in the next chapter.)

Some moral issues are relatively easy to answer on Christian principles—e.g. whether to allow abortion-on-demand and euthanasia-on-demand and clear cases of racial discrimination—even if they are difficult to implement. But others involve a complexity that requires great political, military, social, linguistic, and economic judgments. Further, these issues can be looked at from different angles and with different interests being involved. In these situations (e.g. the best way to keep the peace between East and West and the related issues of unilateral or multilateral nuclear disarmament) human finitude and sinfulness take their toll and ensure that no single person wholly understands the issue in its fullness or is able to make a perfectly impartial judgment about it. However, we have to make moral decisions in our present state—we cannot wait until we are perfect in heaven above. This being the case, it is obvious that we shall have to expect and live with the reality of Christians coming to different moral conclusions. As Christians we must respect each other as children of God and be ready in that light to discuss and debate the issues.

If Christians are not sure what they ought to do in every issue that faces their society, they ought to be sure about one thing—that it is their duty to pray. This is what Paul told Timothy so that he in turn could teach it to the churches:

> First of all, then, I urge that supplications, prayers, intercessions, and thanksgivings be made for all men, for kings and all who are in high positions, that we may lead a quiet and peaceable life, godly and respectful in every way. This is good and acceptable in the sight of God our Saviour, who desires all men to be saved and to come to the knowledge of the truth (1 Tim 2:1-4).

The Roman Empire was not a democratic society and so prayer was often the *only* thing that Christians could do for the government, apart from obeying its laws. The fact that we live in a society where we can take political action to set up and bring down governments does not mean we should pray the less. Indeed we should pray the more. But is the ministry of intercession taken seriously in our churches? Do we make vague requests of God and leave it there? Or do we prepare to address God on the issues of our time by making sure we are aware of them and by believing that God is really interested in the promotion of justice and mercy in his world? It is a rule of the spiritual life that the mind functions better in making moral judgments when it prays. But so often we merely take our agenda from the (humanist) media and bring it to God and leave it there. We do not view the world with eyes that have learned from God's Word the principles of justice and mercy, righteousness and compassion, and then in that light make our supplications, prayers and intercessions for all men, and especially for those who hold high office in government, trade, industry, commerce, education, the media and so on. There is much room for spiritual and moral progress in the ministry of intercession within the churches.

In a little book like this it is not feasible to go into any of the moral issues within society and the world in detail. And to say a little is dangerous! But I would say that there is a duty of conscience laid upon each local church to consider seriously what love for the neighbor means in terms of serving the local community. Evangelism and political/social service are not totally different areas of Christian mission for they flow into and out of each other. People have bodies as well as souls and in their bodies they live in specific places amongst other people. The church cannot merely think of saving the soul. It has to think of the well being of the whole person in the total context. So it is that the church cannot avoid involvement (on God's side in the work of his kingdom of love and justice) in the practical issues of society.

8

Conscience as Sovereign

We are all familiar with the distinction between the legislature and the judiciary. This distinction is basic for civilized countries. If we make use of this to describe conscience then we can say that the legislator is Christ the Lord and the Christian conscience is the judge.

When your conscience is rightly functioning it takes a position as if it were outside you (though it is a part of you) and pronounces for or against you in accordance with God's will (as you have learned it). It does this without giving any reasons: it is categorical. And it judges without any concessions or allowances: it is absolute. Furthermore, your conscience only judges you—your thoughts, feelings and actions—not those of anyone else: and when it has delivered its judgment there is no appeal against it. This is why moral theologians in days past talked of conscience as *invincible* (meaning that it speaks the ultimate authoritative word and is incontrovertible) and they coined the statement *conscientia semper sequenda* (conscience is always to be followed).

TESTING CLAIMS

Always to obey conscience is fine but such a procedure can be abused! In the name of conscience, people can and do claim to do all kinds of things (often today, the very opposite of what for centuries has been regarded as right). So, we are not surprised to learn that while maintaining this absolute right of conscience, Christian theologians have provided various tests to be applied in order that a person who claims to act according to conscience may be able to check his or her motivation. The two basic sources of danger, involved in judgments of conscience, are human finitude and human sinfulness. We are limited in what we know and can know: we can only see a part of any totality. Only God is all-knowing. Then our sinfulness can cloud or blur our knowledge and vision without our realizing it.

Regrettably, in modern church life tests of conscience are rarely mentioned or used. Here are some basic tests:

1. Have I done my utmost to check what is the teaching of the Scriptures and what has been the teaching of the Church over the centuries in this area which concerns me?

2. Have I been obedient as a Christian (as far as I know myself) up to this point of time in that I have obeyed my conscience and where I have failed I have confessed my sins to God? Have I had and do I have a good conscience?

3. Have I done all I can to work out what will be the consequences of my actions both for myself and for others if I follow in this matter what I think is the dictate of conscience?

4. Have I discussed the matter fully with a trusted, wiser friend?

5. And, having carefully done what 1 through 3 require do I feel any trace of shame or uneasiness as I think about acting according to what I think is the voice of my conscience?

If faithfully applied, these tests help to remove the possibility that a person, when claiming to follow conscience, is in fact following fancy, or prejudice, obstinacy or pride. And they are most useful when the action contemplated is very different from what Christians normally do.

Let us take a couple of examples. The first example is from the 'age of conscience', the seventeenth century. Take the case of one of the Puritan ministers of the Church of England, e.g. Richard Baxter, or John Owen, as he faced the question between 1660 and 1662 as to whether he would follow certain procedures required by King Charles II before he could officially minister within that Church as an ordained priest. One issue was whether or not to make a public statement that the Book of Common Prayer (1559: revised 1662) contained nothing that was contrary to the written Word of God. These Puritans took the command 'not to bear false witness' seriously, and because they had reservations about small things, here and there, in the collection of services of the Book, they were unable to take the oath. They did not act hastily or without consultation. They knew that they were probably committing themselves to lives of poverty and hardship and they felt no shame in becoming (as they were called) Nonconformists. In this case, the king and his government placed excessively demanding and unnecessary requirements on men whom they knew to have tender consciences and the result was the birth of English Nonconformity. But the Puritans, who did not conform, seem to have followed these (or similar) tests and so they had no option but to follow their consciences and cease to be clergy of the National Church.

Now an example from the modern scene. It is of a Christian woman who is married, has two fine children, has just got a good job, and finds herself pregnant. She tells herself that the Lord has guided her into this job, that she needs a job for personal satisfaction in life, that the family needs the money to put the children through college, and that she is really too old at thirty-eight to have another baby. So she talks to her husband and persuades him that she ought to have an abortion. She persuades herself that other women do this, that it is a quick and easy clinical operation, and that no one will ever know about it. However, if she does speak to her pastor or to some wise Christian friend, then perhaps he or she would probably put these (or similar) tests to her, so that she can check whether she is doing God's will. In this case, just to begin the process of asking the questions and thus applying the tests is to raise serious doubts, and it is possible that if she is a sincere Christian she will change her mind about the abortion.

The claim of an invincible conscience also occurs with reference to 'charismatic' claims. Take the example of the young man of around twenty who believes he has been baptized in/with the Holy Spirit, and who makes such a claim as: 'The Lord is leading me to give up college and to go and live in a Christian commune in California.' Let us suppose that he is a person who is constantly reading his Bible and praying to the Lord and that he really believes that the Spirit of the Lord has directed him in this way. Experience teaches that it is very difficult to be sure that one is led directly by the Lord (and when one is young, enthusiastic, inexperienced, gullible and impressionable, it is easy to mistake imagination, desire or fancy for the leading of the Spirit). But, again, if this young man is ready to talk, then the application of these (or similar) tests will at least provide him with the opportunity of checking by some objective criteria what he feels he ought to do. He may, for example, be able to recognize (in applying test 3) that by leaving college he is not merely throwing away opportunities which may not easily come again but also bringing grief and pain to his parents, whom the Lord certainly wants him to honor.

The reason for applying tests is to help the people of God be truly the people of God in terms of their obedience of the Lord. They are not meant to stop a person following his conscience. Rather, they are to ensure that when he does, it is truly his conscience and nothing else that he is following. As secularist humanism and pragmatism gain ground in western society, Christians will find that they are having to follow their consciences much more than they have in the past. Thus the great need, as we often have emphasized, is that they have educated consciences which are sensitive to the Lord, and know how to check that it is conscience that they are obeying.

RESISTING CONSCIENCE

If one problem in the Church is the facing of the results of the immature, sovereign conscience, another is that of the silenced conscience. In matters of straightforward moral commitment, some Christian people decide not to obey the voice of conscience. The spiritual and moral temperature of Christian families and churches is often lowered because some people make a decision to reject the dictates of conscience when demands are made that hurt.

Conscience raises its voice within you without you asking or desiring that this should be so. You recognize your duty, but, of course, there is an intimate connection between your conscience and your will. While you cannot at first easily stop your conscience telling you what your duty is, you can *will* not to do what you ought to do. Spiritual growth occurs when the conscience and the will are in harmony. As the lungs need air to breathe and as they develop by the constant inhaling and exhaling of breath, so your conscience grows in its capacity to tell you the Lord's will as you actually obey what you are told.

At first it is difficult for a Christian to disobey conscience for the experience is painful, but if the resistance to the voice of conscience becomes a regular feature of your moral experience, then the voice of conscience will gradually become ever weaker and will virtually die. It will be like the sound from a radio which has burnt-out batteries.

There are many Christians who go so far in their spiritual and moral pilgrimage with Jesus as their guide, and then they realize that to go further will take them a long way from the familiar, the socially acceptable, and the normal. There will have to be changes in habits, use of time, money and so on. They way of the cross becomes a threat to the easy life-style. To follow conscience further will be to rock the boat. To obey the Lord will be divisive in the family, among friends or in the peer group.

People silence the voice of conscience in a variety of ways. Some begin to think of apparently good explanations of why they have to stay with their present life-style and stage of Christian maturity. A married woman, for example, whose husband is not a believer, may tell you that she cannot commit herself any more to Christian discipleship for to go further in obedience will rock her marriage and cause tensions which she has no desire to face. In a time of a high divorce rate such reasoning is plausible—but not at the judgment seat of Christ!

Other people run away from the voice of conscience by engaging in a multitude of activities (many of them useful to the community) or by taking on extra paid work. Such people will not sit still or be quiet (the thought of a quiet day for prayer or a retreat for meditation frightens them) because when they do sit still for long enough they cannot face their thoughts and their consciences. Yet others turn to the bottle to drown the reality of conscience in the lake of alcohol. In our day alcoholism is a serious problem in society and some of it arises from this escape from conscience.

A long time ago the prophet, Jeremiah, declared that 'the heart is deceitful above all things, and desperately corrupt; who can understand it?' (17:9). The reality of the sinful nature (which remains even in Christians) and the incitement of the devil and the materialistic culture, combine to delude people into justifying their rejection of the voice of conscience. And, as can be seen from the case of the excessively religious Pharisees, whose religion Jesus thoroughly condemned, it is possible to turn to external, self-justifying religious deeds and public service as a way of escaping from the call of conscience to internal purity of heart and external deeds of love. The words of Jesus in Matthew 23 uttered in the first century are still as searching today in our very different religious and cultural situation. He castigated the practice of emphasizing minor religious duties and neglecting 'the weightier matters of the law, justice and mercy and faith'. And he talked of the practice of cleansing the outside of the cup and leaving the inside filthy: 'You appear outwardly righteous to men, but within you are full of hypocrisy'. Deafening conscience is one route to hypocrisy.

To reject continually the voice of conscience is, in the language of the Bible to 'harden the heart' (e.g. Rom 11:7; Eph 4:18; Heb 3:13,15). This is the condition of some people before they are converted to God through Christ by the Holy Spirit. Regrettably, it can also become the lot of the Christian if there is persistent rejection of the voice of conscience. Here, words from the Letter to the Hebrews are salutary.

> For it is impossible to restore again to repentance those who have once been enlightened, who have tasted the heavenly gift, and have become partakers of the Holy Spirit, and have tasted the goodness of the word of God and the powers of the age to come, if they then commit apostasy, since they crucify the Son of God on their own account and hold him up to contempt (6:4–6).

Partially committed Christians reveal that their loyalty to Christ is minimal by their attitudes and actions. Thus they do not promote the cause of the Gospel. And their own spiritual state is, to say the least, dangerous.

9

The Function of Conscience

The education and formation of the conscience is a continuing process, only ending at death. Until then the Christian is a pupil in the school of Christ. Conscience does not wait to function until it is suitably educated in Christian truth. Under the influence of the indwelling Spirit of the Lord, the conscience of the believer is always active and the believer is disposed, by grace, to obey its dictates. But the fact of this disposition does not mean that there is no conflict within the heart of the Christian. Belonging as he does to two worlds, and having two natures, the Christian often experiences a war within himself. The, old, sinful nature resists the promptings of the conscience and the Holy Spirit, and so to walk in the way of the Lord demands determination and persistence of will.

To be aware of how conscience works within the believer should help you to understand more of the grace and work of God within you, as you work out your salvation in awe and with reverence (Phil. 2:12). Here in five statements is a summary of the function of conscience:

1. *Conscience guides you to do God's will in each situation you face in your life.* As you go through each new day and the varied situations in it, you will feel that you ought to do this and it is your duty to do that. Of course, in general things you will find that your duty is the same every day—e.g. to be at work on time, to find a period of

the day for personal prayer and meditation, to care for your family, and to respect the dignity of each person you meet.

But, apart from your conscience directing you to fulfill your basic obligations, there will be varied situations in which you will be forced to make a moral choice—e.g. in what you say on the telephone, in what you write in a letter, in a conversation over lunch, and how you treat a child. You will recognize it as a situation of moral choice for there will be at least two alternative actions that you can take. You will find yourself bringing to bear on the situation principles that you have learned from the Bible and Christian teaching and applying them in that situation. You will feel a desire to do what God loves, and avoid what he hates, but you may also feel tempted to take an easy way out of the situation. Your decision will be taken after you have worked out as far as you are able to the consequences of each of the alternative choices. However, once your conscience has come to a judgment as to what is right then you will feel certain that it is this and not that thing which you ought to do.

Some choices are relatively straightforward and you do not need to linger long before your conscience declares what is your duty. For example, you may be a member of a society or sports club which makes a decision to have its activity at the same time as your church has its Sunday worship. Here your conscience will quickly tell you that your first duty is to worship and serve the Lord your God and that you must hallow the Lord's Day.

Other choices are more complex. Take the case of a secretary who is paid to work—i.e. to do what her boss asks her to do. When she answers the phone and greets visitors to the office, she is not answering and greeting in her own capacity as an individual female, but she is functioning as the representative of her boss. This means that she may well have to do and say things in the name of the boss and his company which she would not do or say if she were acting solely in her own name. For example, she may regularly be faced with the request from her boss that she tells other people what she knows to be lies or at best half-truths. In facing this type of situation she cannot simply apply the principle that it is wrong to lie and therefore refuse to do what he says. Her moral reason tells her that in her employment she is only speaking in his name and for him and so it is he who is telling the lie not she. So her conscience may direct her to do and say what he wants, but she will do it with a heavy heart, even if she puts on a cheerful face. She is, of course, free to speak to her boss about this kind of thing and seek to help him to modify his requests, and she is also free to leave that job. But this situation is obviously not a simple case of right and wrong.

Or take the situation where it is a choice not between right and wrong, but between different degrees of right. The Christian often faces situations which call for decision and action: not to act would be sinful, a sin of omission; but, to act halfheartedly would also be a sin, this time a sin of commission. Let us take this example. Your conscience speaks to you of the duty to give a gift to a Christian College, which is raising money for a new library. You believe you can satisfy your conscience by giving $50, but deep down inside you, there is the compelling feeling that you should give $75, and your moral reason tells you that you can just about afford the larger sum. Here, to follow conscience aright is to give the larger sum. It is the best of two right possibilities.

> George Herbert wrote:
> Teach me, my God and King,
> In all things Thee to see;
> And what I do in anything
> To do it as for Thee.

Such a spirit of service and commitment includes a sensitive conscience!

2. *Conscience judges you by the highest standards it knows, the will of God.* Whatever be your profoundest and deepest comprehension of the will of God, it is by this that your conscience will judge you. And the judgment is not only of what you have done but also of what you have failed to do. Further it is not merely of actions but also of motives and secret thoughts. This work of conscience is more searching and comprehensive in its judgment of you.

However, quite amazingly, since by divine grace you are a child of God and love God and his law, there is a ready welcome in your heart for this continual judgment. A part of you (your old nature) sometimes resists and rebels making you feel disturbed and confused within; but you know, deep within yourself, that your conscience is right and you welcome it. This was the experience of the psalmist:

> Search me, O God, and know my heart!
> Try me and know my thoughts!
> And see if there be aby wicked way in me,

and lead me in the way everlasting. (Psalm 139:23-4)
The function of your conscience as judge may be triggered into action by all kinds of things—e.g. a sermon, a prayer, or a television program. As you grow in Christian maturity you welcome this searching of your heart and this trying of your thoughts. In the words of Samuel Arnold your daily prayer will be:

> Show me, as my soul can bear,
>   The depth of inbred sin;
> All the unbelief declare,
>   The pride that lurks within;
> Take me, whom thyself hast bought,
>   Bring into captivity
> Every high aspiring thought
>   That would not stoop to thee.

It is a good practice to end each day with self-examination, allowing your conscience to speak as you survey that day that is past.

3. *Conscience causes you to have a sense of guilt, a pain of heart.* Since conscience is the judge that exists to promote the right, it has the power to make you feel pain—not physical but nevertheless real pain and grief in your soul. This occurs as you accept the judgment concerning your guilt and recognize that you have not done what you ought to have done. You realize that you have not only hurt yourself but you have also grieved the Lord who loves you.

In chapter five we distinguished different types of guilt. It is important to remember that the informed conscience only causes you to feel guilty because of sin; it does not make you feel guilty for not being or doing what your parent, teacher, professor or godmother imposed and impressed upon you a long time ago (unless this is truly God's will). In the words of an old Methodist hymn, conscience functions in such a way as to make you say, as you see your sin:

> O that I could repent,
>   With all my idols part
> And to thy gracious eye present
>   A humble, contrite heart.
> A heart with grief oppressed,
>   For having grieved my God
> A troubled heart that cannot rest,
>   Till sprinkled with thy blood.

The pain of heart which is felt by the Christian conscience is not self pity, but grief for offending the Lord.

4. *Conscience points you to Christ, the Saviour.* By constantly and consistently placing before the mind of the believer the moral implications of the will of God for his life, the conscience also necessarily points to Christ. For Christ is both the One who perfectly obeyed the will of the Lord and at the same time became (to remain) the Saviour of the world. So the conscience in its function as judge points to Christ for deliverance and pardon; and, functioning as guide, it points to him as the perfectly obedient Servant of the Lord, and the example for all to follow.

Your Christian life may be described with various metaphors and images—pilgrimage, discipleship, spiritual warfare and priestly service. From the perspective of the function of the conscience, it may be described in terms of a constant turning from the recognition of guilt for sin to the mercy of the Saviour from sin. The Christian Gospel calls for repentance and faith to begin the Christian life: it also calls for continuing repentance and faith within the Christian life. This pattern of penitence and faith is built into the structure of the Christian life and is expressed in your daily (evening) quiet time of prayer and in the services of worship used in churches. For example, all services in Anglicanism—Morning and Evening Prayer and the Eucharist—contain the confession of sins, the turning from them to Christ, the absolution and the determination to forsake them and go forth in Christ's name and power to serve God in his world.

The believer with an active conscience longs (to use Charles Wesley's words):

> O for a heart to praise my God,
>   A heart from sin set free
> A heart that always feels thy blood
>   So freely spilt for me.
> A heart resigned, submissive, meek,
>   My great Redeemer's throne,
> Where only Christ is heard to speak,
>   Where Jesus reigns alone.

Distress of conscience leads to a lively faith in Christ. The Christian conscience has a built-in bias toward Christ—because the Holy Spirit dwells in the heart.

5. *Conscience witnesses that you are living by faith and in faithfulness.* In chapter three we noted that Paul claimed to have a 'clear' and a 'good' conscience. Also he urged his converts to aim, by God's grace, to have the same experience—'they must hold the mystery of the faith with a clear conscience' (1 Tim 3:9). In the First Letter of John the expression 'we know . . .' is significant for it points to Christian assurance. 'By this we know that we abide in God and God in us because he has given us of his own Spirit' (4:13); 'We know that we have passed out of death into life because we love the brethren ' (3:14) and 'We know that we are of God and the whole world is in the power of the evil one' (5:19). Here is the conscience witnessing that those who truly believe and live in the light of their faith belong to God. Thus conscience works in harmony with the indwelling Spirit to bring that sense of assurance—so well expressed in the hymns of Charles Wesley.

My God, I am Thine;
  What a comfort divine,
What a blessing to know that my Jesus is mine!
  In the heavenly Lamb
  Thrice happy I am,
And my heart it doth dance at the sound of his name.

Regrettably this concept of the good conscience has been all but eclipsed from the life of the churches.

10

Free to Obey

There is a noticeable external difference between the child who obeys his parent willingly and gladly and the child who obeys reluctantly and grudingly. Also, internally, each child has a different complex of feelings.

Likewise, in situations where the will of the Lord is reasonably clear, we may say that there are two kinds of Christians. There are those who obey the Lord willingly and gladly, and others who recognize they should obey but view the prospect with hesitation and reluctance. To put it another way, there are some Christians whose consciences tell them what they ought to do and they feel both free and desirous of doing it to please the Lord, and there are others whose consciences tell them what is their duty but who feel a reluctance and little desire to do what they know is right. In one case Christian freedom is known and in the other there is still bondage, for obedience is a burden.

Addressing both Jews and Gentiles in Galatia, St. Paul wrote of moral and spiritual freedom: 'For freedom Christ has set us free: stand fast, therefore, and do not submit again to the yoke of slavery' (5:1). And he added that 'you were called to freedom, brethren; only do not use your freedom as an opportunity for the flesh, but through love be servants of one another' (5:13). It is clear that for Paul freedom is both the indicative (the objective reality) and the imperative (that at which to aim) of the Christian life. In Christ, who is his Representative, the Christian is totally free and bears the name of child of God: in the rough and tumble of daily life, this freedom is to be experienced and maintained, never being allowed to escape from his vision. Obviously freedom has both negative aspects (freedom from) and positive aspects (freedom for/into). These will emerge as we examine Christian freedom.

1. *Christian freedom is not freedom from your physical body or your human connections and relationships.* St. Paul claimed to enjoy the freedom of Christ but this did not change the fact that he was a Jew and a Roman citizen, that he had to live with pain and tiredness and in relations with people, organizations and government officials. If you owe a bank $1,000 you are not set free from that debt: if you have to fulfil further requirements to get your degree, you are not set free from them: and if you have a family to support you are not released from that obligation.

This point is clearly made in the New Testament where to become a Christian did not make a slave into a freeman. In the Roman Empire slavery was a prominent aspect of society. In any city slaves could comprise up to one third of the total population. Slaves worked in household, on plantations and farms, in ships, on public works and in many small businesses. They could be bought and sold as we buy and sell houses or cars. St. Paul had to accept this situation and he sought to sweeten the relationship of master and slave by bringing the love of Christ into it. 'Let those who are under the yoke of slavery regard their masters as worthy of all honor, so that the name of God and the teaching may not be defamed' (1 Tim 6:2; cf. Col 4:1). However, Paul insisted that in the church such a barrier had no moral basis and was eliminated in Christ—'in Christ there is neither slave nor free...' (Gal 3:28). And he taught that Christian freedom was the indicative and imperative of the Christian life even for the bondservant/slave.

Whatever Christian freedom is, it is not a liberation from your basic lot and position in life as a member of the human community. Christian freedom certainly has its effects upon your whole life, but these do not include changing your basic identity and connections within God's world. A slave may be set free by his master and you may be given a luxurious house in an attractive place; yet in neither case is the change a direct result of your Christian freedom. The voice of Christian freedom is: 'I have learned in whatever state I am to be content. I know how to be abased and I know how to abound ...' (Phil 4:11).

2. *Christian freedom is not freedom from your sinful nature, nor from the ability to sin, nor from the obligation to repent of sin.* The Christian belongs to two worlds and two kingdoms. Your human body points to your membership of this world and the kingdoms of men. Your salvation points to heaven and the kingdom of God. Correspondingly you have two natures. One is the basic, sinful human nature which has been with you since your mother's womb; the other was imparted by the Holy Spirit when you were born from above (John 3:1–11). So there is within you the potential for following the way of the Lord as well as the potential for submitting to the temptations of the world, the flesh and the devil. As a Christian you will not habitually sin, but you are not delivered from the possibility of committing sin, only from the necessity of committing sin. And you must always face up to the need to repent of sin and seek God's forgiveness throughout your Christian life.

3. *Christian freedom is freedom from condemnation before God, the Judge: it is freedom from condemnation for breaking his moral law/commandments.* Before God as Judge you stand condemned if you stand alone for you have failed to obey his commandments both in your inner motivation and in your deeds. However, if you stand there with Christ as your Substitute and Representative, resting in his vicarious humanity, then you are pronounced righteous for Christ's sake. Indeed, God's verdict is not that you are 'not guilty' (for you are guilty) but it is that you are accepted, forgiven and welcomed because Christ has himself, as your Saviour, borne the condemnation for your guilt that you deserve. 'Christ gave himself for our sins to deliver us from the present evil age, according to the will of our God and Father' (Gal 1:4). Christian freedom is being placed by God in a right relationship with himself through Jesus Christ. This is another way of stating that you are justified by faith—declared righteous in God's court because of your Advocate, Jesus.

'There is, therefore, now no condemnation for those who are in Christ Jesus' (Rom 8:1) for they are set free 'from the law of sin and death' (Rom 8:2). No wonder Paul exclaimed: 'If God is for us, who is against us? He who did not spare his own Son but gave him up for us all, will he not also give us all things with him? Who shall lay any charge against God's elect? It is God who justifies; who is to condemn? Is it Christ Jesus, who died, yes, who was raised from the dead, who is at the right hand of God, who indeed intercedes for us?' (Rom 8:31–4).

4. *Christian freedom is freedom from the obligation and effort to earn your salvation by what you do in your efforts to keep God's law.* There are two ways to heaven. One is the way of perfect obedience to the law of God, perfect submission to the divine will. This was the way Christ took and he was sinless. The other is the way of grace, and the way of faith. It is the route that is based on the fact that Jesus is the way, truth and life and no one comes to the Father except through him. It is the life that looks to Jesus as the pioneer and perfecter of faith.

Many Christians find this truth too good to be true or too amazing to accept. They give lip service to it but still secretly hold the view that they are to earn their way into God's favor by their good deeds. Christian freedom is the release from all such thinking: it is believing deep in your heart the impossible—that salvation is by grace and by grace alone. Such belief is really possible because the God who pronounces you righteous in his heavenly court is the Lord who places his Spirit in your heart. The new birth (regeneration) and forgiveness/acceptance (justification) belong together in God's treatment of his children.

5. *Christian freedom is freedom to serve and love God, with joy and peace.* Some people always draw the wrong conclusions from what they hear or read. All of us have met such people. Paul had to face the problem (and so did James by the evidence of his Epistle) of some Christians who thought that since they were saved both from the condemnation of the Law and from the Law as a route to heaven, they could think and do whatever they liked. In the church in Corinth certain members said, 'I am allowed to do anything' (1 Cor 6:12; 10:23). In the church at Rome there was the same possibility and so Paul asked: 'What then? Are we to sin because we are not under law but under grace?' In reply to such talk he made use of the analogy of the slave market where slaves were sold and bought. He emphasized that freedom from the Law (the old master) does not mean freedom to do anything or everything. For, in being set free from one master's control, the person is bought by another. And, as St. Peter insisted, Christians have been bought with a price, a price far beyond that of the best silver and gold—even the precious, sacrificial blood of Jesus (1 Pet 1:19). Or, returning to St. Paul: 'But now that you have been set free from sin and have become slaves of God, the return you get is sanctification and its end, eternal life' (Rom 6:22). In becoming a Christian we gain a new master, even the Lord Jesus and he has his own standards.

St. Mark records the answer of Jesus to the question from a Jewish expert in the Law of Moses:
> One of the scribes asked him, 'Which commandment is the first of all?' Jesus answered, 'The first is, "Hear O Israel: The Lord our God, the Lord is one; and you shall love the Lord your God with all your heart, and with all your soul, and with all your mind, and with all your strength." The second is this, "You shall love your neighbor as yourself". There is no other commandment greater than these.' (12:28-31).

When you ask yourself, 'How do I love myself?' your answer will be either 'selfishly' or 'I find it hard to love myself'. Thus the loving of the neighbor appears impractical.

'To love myself' means that I know and feel that I am in charge of my body, mind and feelings. It is to know that I am an individual person, having integrity, meaning and purpose. And it is to follow my own conscience.

Further, to love myself is to accept myself with all that is mine—my figure, looks, personality, skills (or lack of them), work and family. It is to feel good about myself. It is to have self-esteem.

In the light of the fact that I am a justified sinner, whom God has accepted for Christ's sake, it is to accept myself as God has also accepted me. Even as each of us comes to Jesus 'Just as I am . . .' (as the well-known hymn puts it), so each of us loves himself by accepting himself as he is, as the child of God, as made in the image of God, as lovable, as a forgiven sinner, as a potential saint. Accepting yourself as God has accepted you, releases you from worry about yourself and drives away the feelings of scorn or hatred that you may have for yourself. Thus you are set free to love God and your neighbor as you are, enabled by the guiding and strengthening of the indwelling Spirit of God. You are not diverted by anxiety, fear or misguided zeal; and feelings of being hurt, upset, slighted or rejected do not stand in the way.

Therefore you love your neighbor because of what he is in God's estimation and because God has put love for him in your heart. Jesus gave content to this freedom to love when, after he had taken the role of a slave and washed the sweaty and dirty feet of his disciples, he said: 'A new commandment I give to you, that you love one another; even as I have loved you, that you also love one another. By this all men will know that you are my disciples, if you have love, one for another' (John 13:34-5). And later he repeated this teaching: 'This is my commandment, that you love one another as I have loved you. Greater love has no man than this, that a man lays down his life for his friends' (15:12). This said, he prepared to go to his death at Calvary.

The example of Jesus lifts the Christian life above the mere keeping of rules or the mere obeying of laws. Though including this aspect, it sets life upon a plane in which, by the power of the indwelling Spirit, the disciple, like his Lord and Master, begins to exemplify in action what love for others is all about. Love can never be adequately defined (but 1 Corinthians 13 and 1 John 4:7-10 help), and this is why Jesus called upon his disciples to follow his example. Also this is why, in the education of conscience, the example of Christ as well as that of the apostles (and the saints through the centuries) is very important. The Christian life cannot be reduced to a set of rules for that would produce a barren legalism. On the other hand, the Christian life cannot be defined without reference to obeying commandments for that would produce antinomianism. The Christian life is a life of serving and loving God and the neighbor under the direction of Christ, the Lord, who brings to us not only his salvation but also his example and the Law of God. In this sense we can talk as did the Puritans of the 'grace of law'. Under Christ the Lord and Saviour we obey the commandments.

The teaching of St. Paul dovetails with that of his Master. Those who are Christ's disciples are to live by Christ's commandments; set free from the power of sin, they are to love God and man:

> Owe no man anything, except to love one another; for he who loves his neighbor has fulfilled the law. The commandments, 'You shall not commit adultery, You shall not kill, You shall not steal, You shall not covet', and any other commandment, are summed up in the sentence, 'You shall love your neighbor as yourself.' Love does no wrong to the neighbor; therefore love is the fulfilling of the law (Rom 13:8-10).

By loving the neighbor as Christ loved his disciples, you will not earn your salvation. Rather, by loving the neighbor through the love of God which has been poured into your heart, you show that you are both a recipient and channel of the love of God. If your love for others then fulfils the moral law of God, you realize that it is not your own merely human love, but the love of God which is in you.

6. *Christian freedom means freedom of choice in matters that are nonessentials as far as salvation and the love of God are concerned.* There is within

most of us the tendency to major on minors and to make minors into majors. We get worked up or irate about the indifferent matter and remain virtually unconcerned by the major matter. To preach that the drinking of beer or wine with a meal is a sin of the same order as telling lies is to have a confused mind. To insist that a particular way of dressing (e.g. the wearing of slacks by women) is a sin of the same order as fornication is also to have a confused mind. To say that the wearing of particular vestments is necessary by the minister in order for a Eucharist to be a means of grace is to get things out of perpective. To claim that God's Word is only found in one translation (eg. KJV) is to have a closed mind. To insist that nonessentials are as important as essentials is to confuse the conscience.

In the early years of the Protestant Reformation, when there was great enthusiasm to get things right and to obey the Lord wholly, John Calvin of Geneva recognized that the binding of the conscience with 'things indifferent' was a real danger for Protestants. In his great work, *Institutes of the Christian Religion* he had this to say:

> Regarding outward things that are of themselves indifferent *(adiaphora)*, we are not bound before God by any religious obligation preventing us from sometimes using them and other times not using them, indifferently. And the knowledge of this freedom is very necessary for us, for if it is lacking, our consciences will have no repose and there will be no end to superstitions. Today we seem to many to be unreasonable because we stir up discussion over the unrestricted eating of meat, use of holidays and of vestments, and such things, which seem to them vain frivolities.
>
> But these matters are more important than is commonly believed. For when consciences once ensnare themselves, they enter a long and inextricable maze, not easy to get out of. If a man begins to doubt whether he may use linen for sheets, shirts, handkerchiefs, and napkins, he will afterward be uncertain also about hemp; finally doubt will arise over tow! For he will turn over in his mind whether he can sup without napkins, or go without a handkerchief. If any man should consider daintier food unlawful, in the end he will not be at peace before God, when he eats either black bread or common victuals, while it occurs to him that he could sustain his body on even coarser foods. If he boggles at sweet wine, he will not dare touch water if sweeter and cleaner than other water. To sum up, he will come to the point of considering it wrong to step upon a straw across his path, as the saying goes (III:xix:7).

Even as certain forms of late medieval religion had caused people to fall into the trap of scrupulosity, so Calvin knew that there was always a danger of any kind of religious person falling into this same trap. Protestants could fall into it by being bound by the strong views of a person they respect, by following uncontrolled imagination, by imposing moral burdens which have no basis in God's moral law and by other ways. The spiritual dangers of this majoring on minors or this scrupulosity were seen by Calvin as either a descent into despair, or of throwing aside all restraint and plunging into immorality.

There are, of course, occasions when Christians are not free to exercise the liberty that they have in Christ. This is because (as we saw in looking at 1 Corinthians 8 & 10 in chapter 3) love for others in the church causes us to act according to their consciences rather than our own. But, though you are to limit your freedom when the integrity of a weaker fellow Christian is concerned, you must excercise your liberty when the challenge comes from the Pharisaic spirit, for this spirit wants to bring everyone back into the very bondage from which Christ has released us. To quote Calvin again as he commented on 1 Corinthians 10:29, 'The soul of a pious man looks exclusively to the tribunal of God, has no regard for man, is satisfied with the blessing of liberty secured for it by Christ, and is bound to no individuals, and to no circumstances of time and place.'

A well trained, a perfectly formed and a thoroughly-educated conscience is only possible in the Christian who is standing fast in the freedom gained for him by Christ and made real through the presence of the indwelling Spirit. You need not only to know what to do but you need also to be free to do it. Jesus Christ the Lord both instructs you in his way and sets you free to do it. This is what he once said to Jews who believed in him: 'If you continue in my word, you are truly my disciples, and you will know the truth, and the truth will make you free' (John 8:31). Then he pointed out that truth comes from the Son: in fact Truth is the Son, and so 'if the Son makes you free, you will be free indeed' (8:36).

Epilogue

For the honor and glory of God, Christians must educate not only their consciences but also those of all people. For the sake of Western civilization, Christians must train their consciences and those of others. The Church in the West, and the West itself, face a moral and spiritual crisis and action is needed immediately.

In *The Times* of London of September 10, 1983, there appeared a short article by Professor R. P. C. Hanson entitled "Wanted: a modern medievalism". A recent visit to Rome had made the professor reflect on the relationship of Christianity and Western civilization, beginning with the conversion of Constantine the Great in the year 312. During the long period we call the Middle Ages 'society and civilization were permeated and infused with Christianity, for better or for worse with both good and bad results. They were the ages of faith, faith triumphant, faith confident, faith everywhere accepted without question, faith abused, misplaced, misunderstood and exploited, but certainly faith, Christian faith.'

Of course Christianity adapted to the slowly changing society of those centuries—barbarian successor-kingdoms to that of Rome, feudal society, independent city-states and the birth of the nation state. In this process Christianity changed much and suffered much but 'it supplied the values and moral basis and ideals by which medieval society existed. It was indeed a society steeped in Christianity.' Regrettably the ages of faith have passed.

However, Christianity as a faith for the whole world is neither decaying nor collapsing. It has shown a remarkable tenacity, vigor and adaptability in all continents and it will continue to do so. Yet it is true that Christianity 'does not dominate, permeate society in anything like the same way that it did in the Middle Ages. It is not close to the consciousness of men and women in the twentieth century as it was in, say, the twelfth. It does not create their world view, supply their morality, provide the framework for their lives. It does not give them those values and assumptions by which they live, which probably must be present in some form in every civilization.'

The professor moves on to ask what performs the function for twentieth-century Western people that Christianity did for their ancestors. Marxism is obviously one answer and it is a creed that supplies moral values and social assumptions. But what of those who are not Marxists and not committed Christians. What are the moral values, basic beliefs and world outlook which lie behind the thinking and behavior of modern Westerners? To this he replies:

> The answer must be that no single all-embracing ideology or creed exists here. All we can detect is a number of disparate assumptions not logically connected with each other: the power of science to discover truth about the physical universe; the dominating necessity of satisfying our physical needs, above all our sexual desire . . . ; the duty of being as tolerant as possible to everybody; complete uncertainty and indifference as to any purpose or obligation or reality perceptible in the universe beyond the immediately psychological and physical needs of the individual person.

In the first chapter I called this general attitude 'secularist humanism'. Hanson states that 'one might describe this ill-assorted collection of principles as a kind of individualistic, positivist, tolerant hedonism'. In other words, science has destroyed metaphysics and there is nothing to do but enjoy oneself with as little trouble to other people as possible.

I wholly agree with Hanson that it is inconceivable that such a philosophy could infuse or sustain a civilization for more than a short time. It is very doubtful whether it can resist the power of Marxism and resurgent Islam. We find that twentieth-century people are like the pagans of the fifth century—balefully aware that their cherished paganism has no power to resist the force of the new advancing faith. So the question we face is: Can Christianity become once more the sustaining genius of a post-Marxist and post-humanist civilization—and what are Christians doing about it?